HOW 10% OF THE PEOPLE GET 90% OF THE PIE

HOW 10% OF THE PEOPLE GET 90% OF THE PIE

CRAIG E. SODERHOLM

St. Martin's Griffin ❧ New York

Originally published by Performance Dynamics in 1994 as *Subliminal Power Persuasion*.

Book design by Anne Scatto/PIXEL PRESS

Library of Congress Cataloging-in-Publication Data

Soderholm, Craig E.
    How 10% of the people get 90% of the pie : get your share
    using subliminal persuasion techniques / Craig E. Soderholm.
       p.   cm.
    Includes bibliographical references.
    ISBN 0-312-15468-2 (pbk.)
    1. Selling—Psychological aspects.   2. Marketing—Psychological
aspects.   3. Consumer behavior.   4. Subliminal advertising.
I. Title.
HF5438.8.P75S65   1997
658.85—dc21   97-8946
                                            CIP

10 9 8 7 6 5 4 3

TO
VICTORIA
AND
ERIC

CONTENTS

INTRODUCTION

Regardless of titles, professions, or lifestyles, we are all attempting to sell ourselves, our ideas, and our opinions every day of our lives. The engineer or architect proposing a design to his client. The clerk asking for a raise. The person who wants to attract that special someone. The teacher impressing upon his class the benefits of an education. The attorney attempting to get her point across to a judge or jury. The police detective attempting to extract information or a confession. The employee trying to get his idea accepted by the company.

Success or failure, the difference between making twenty thousand dollars a year or two hundred thousand, a happy relationship or one doomed to continual arguments or disagreements, depend upon effective persuasion. Unfortunately, it is an art, skill, and science which, while one of the most attempted, is the least understood of all communications tools.

That is why this book was written.

Originally the script for specialized workshops directed to high-income sales professionals, *How 10% of the People Get 90% of the Pie* refutes and ultimately destroys concepts purported as dogma for years. In their place, it reveals successful, field-proven methods of persuasion as well as explanations for why those methods work to enable consistent results for everyone who uses them.

No one knows that better than I because I've been a salesman most of my life. But it wasn't until a very special introduction and subsequent association that I began to realize what a complex and intricate science persuasion really is, the incredible power it wields when properly applied, and the positive benefits which result from its effective, consistent application.

Prior to that, the only thing I knew for sure was the truth of the oldest saying in sales: "Ten percent of the people do ninety percent of the business while the rest scramble for the leftovers." There are those, for example, who have been in sales all their lives and, while they might make a decent living, don't even compare to the supersalespeople who can persuade almost anyone of anything at the drop of a hat. Just looking at the two in actual selling situations, you might not be able to guess which is which. But the end results quickly show they aren't remotely similar.

Why? What was the real difference? Why did those few seem to persuade everyone they talked to while the rest of us had to scrape for anything we could get? Those and a myriad of other questions plagued me and I wanted to find the answers.

I read volumes of books, went to all the "inspirational and

motivational" seminars every sales and career professional has attended at one time or other, and listened to every tape I could get my hands on. I questioned super-successful people. I even questioned clients—those who purchased and those who did not—all to no avail in finding a solid, reasonable solution.

I'd hear things like, "That guy is just a natural-born salesman," and I'd immediately wonder if we were talking about the same man. Knowing him personally, I found him somewhat withdrawn, not especially fond of people, and I wondered how he sold anything. Yet his success was outstanding.

On the other side of the coin, I knew a very attractive, personable young lady who was warm, giving, open, and very sincere. She openly and sincerely loved people and you would think she'd be a natural in sales. Yet she was let go by three different companies, all of whom liked her but simply couldn't afford to keep her as a salesperson.

Trying to get to the bottom of it, I once asked one of the "superstars" if he could tell me the secret of his success, to which he replied, "I think I'm just luckier than most." So I asked him if I could go along on his next presentation. Afterward, I was more confused than ever! He said exactly the same things I did, yet even in an impossible situation, got "lucky" again. So, I remained in that 90 percent category . . . until I met Michael Curtis.

At that time, Mike was a consultant specializing in subliminal motivation and had done extensive work in employee, management, and promotional development for a number of major corporations.

He told me that, based upon behavioral research, he was

able to determine how people formed opinions, what stimulated them to take immediate action, and the real reasons they purchased certain products as opposed to the reasons they thought or expressed. He claimed to be able, as a result, to construct a profile of successful people and the techniques they used on a consistent basis.

In my profession, knowledge like that would represent a gold mine!

I have to admit, however, that I initially challenged many of the things he said, as others undoubtedly will when reading this book. For years, every sales manager, trainer, seminar, and "motivational" book I had ever read emphasized the things you absolutely must do and those you must avoid. Suddenly someone comes along contradicting the most basic concepts as having no application whatsoever to contemporary society and I had difficulty accepting it.

So we decided to put to the test, in actual tape-recorded selling situations, what I had challenged as little more than outlandish theories, contrasting them against the supposed "tried and true" methods . . . with amazing results.

Those concepts and techniques not only invalidated most of the sales training I'd received, but resulted in the *most successful years of my entire career.*

The most difficult part was breaking the old habits which had become so ingrained. Once that was accomplished, we began in-depth research, some of it in books and tapes I had already seen, but from a totally new perspective. We studied literally hundreds of persuasion techniques, then had the luxury of being able to field-test them in sales situations, constantly expanding our knowledge not only of *what* worked, but more importantly, of *why* certain methods were so effective.

Using those techniques and skills, the barriers and façades people usually put up when talking to a salesperson became transparent. Instant rapport, regardless of personalities, income, or social status was developed with ease. Separating real motivations from those presented as a front or excuse became easier, and determining financial capabilities to purchase what I was offering was no longer a hit-or-miss proposition.

Almost unbelievably, I effected positive, immediate action from those who would otherwise have put off any decision, without employing high-pressure tactics of any kind but rather allowing *them* to come up with the idea.

But most important of all, I was able to use those methods in my personal life and outlook, expanding my understanding of people with an increased ability to see beneath the surface and thereby the freedom to explore new relationships from a perspective I would never have imagined possible.

Strictly for salespeople? Hardly. Because what this book reveals are skills, techniques, and insights which can be used every single day for positive improvement in your career, your life, and your relationships.

Best wishes to you, with the knowledge that you will be embarking on a new and exciting adventure in . . .

SUBLIMINAL POWER PERSUASION

1

THE GURUS

The auditorium of eighty to one hundred men and women seated in semicircular rows before a raised center stage is filled with the drone of conversation. The noise level becomes progressively louder as yet more people in small groups of two and three attempt to find seats together in a room where only a few single chairs are quickly occupied.

When the trickle of latecomers finally ends, a woman at the entrance gives a signal, a lively marching tune blasts from the speakers above the audience, and a man strides from the entrance to the stairs, athletically taking two at a time to reach the stage. The sound of applause quickly drowns out the music as he moves catlike from one end of the stage to the other, flashing a whitened-teeth smile as he, in turn, applauds his audience.

Then, still smiling and quickly scanning the audience row

by row, he slows his own applause and finally clasps his precisely manicured hands together in front of him.

At that signal the applause from the audience tapers off until the room is dead silent and every eye is riveted to the man on stage.

What they see is the epitome of American success. He wears a dark blue $1,000 Giorgio Armani silk suit precisely tailored to fit his trim, athletic physique; a $200 Behar French cuff shirt; a $150 silk Ralph Lauren tie; and $500 Fratelli Rossetti leather wingtips.

In his midforties and sporting a perfectly trimmed mustache, he stands tall and straight, with a casually irresistible allure born in the confidence of having the striking good looks of a Hollywood leading man. And as he surveys the faces of the women in the audience, stopping momentarily on those that are extraordinarily attractive, the thought flashes through his mind that they would probably give anything to be alone with him.

Suddenly, the corners of his mouth twitch into an even wider smile. "Good morning!" his baritone voice almost sings over the speakers. "Is this a great day or what! Lemme hear a YES!"

"Yes!" responds the audience.

"I think I almost heard something a minute ago," he laughs. "Now lemme hear a YES I can really hear!"

"Yes!" responds the audience in a single voice so deafening he can feel the vibration in the stage.

"Now that's finally what I call enthusiasm! That's exciting! And that's what our business is all about because if we don't have enthusiasm and excitement and if we don't create that enthusiasm and excitement in our prospects, we don't make what? Say MONEY!"

"Money!" they shout in unison.

"Let's hear it again! We don't make what?" he shouts, raising his hands in a pose resembling a symphony conductor's.

"Money!" they shout back.

"That's exactly right! And by the way, as long as we're on the subject, how many in this room are here because they want to learn how to make more money? Raise your hands!"

He smiles, looking out over a forest of raised arms.

"That's great! I just wanted to make sure I'm in the right room and obviously, looking at this group of professional men and women, I certainly am!" he exclaims, putting his hands forward, once again applauding his audience as they respond in kind.

"So let's get down to it! I'm here to tell each and every one of you that if you put into practice what you learn over the next few hours, you will absolutely amaze yourself with incredible forces that were dormant within you until today!"

Now, with precise timing, he begins to move quickly back and forth across the stage, while those in the audience know that he is looking directly at each of them.

"I'm going to show you the attitudes that have been holding you back until today! That's right! Until today, you were the only one holding you back, and by the time we're finished, you'll wonder why you didn't see it before! I'm going to show you how to create a need for your product in prospects that will make it impossible for them to refuse you! Find that hard to believe?" he asks, pausing. "Well, you won't by the time we're finished today because you'll learn how to take absolute strangers who walk into your office and within a short time make it impossible for them to turn you down.

"Why? Because you'll be their best friend, that's why! And nobody—I mean nobody—turns down their best friend. Isn't that right! Say YES!"

"Yes!" they respond.

He continues to move swiftly yet smoothly across the stage, scanning the audience.

"When you walk out into that sunshine this afternoon, you'll walk out of here a new person! In fact, your husband or wife may even feel guilty because they'll think they've fallen in love with someone they've never seen before!" he chuckles, as a murmur spreads throughout the audience. "And you know what? In some ways, they'll be right! You came here because you were intelligent enough to know that you had to make changes in your life! Right? Say RIGHT!"

"RIGHT!" they all shout.

"And I can tell just by looking at you that you're going to surprise yourself! Because this is one HELLUVA group of professionals I've got sitting in front of me and each and every one of you deserves success! Now turn to the person on your left and shake their hand, and when you do, say, You deserve success!"

As the entire audience shifts and the sounds of "You deserve success" drift to the stage, he looks over the room, a satisfied smile on his face.

"Now turn to the person on your right, shake their hand and

say, You deserve success!" He pauses. "The reason you deserve it is because each and every one of you is a professional! That's right. You're in the business of closing deals by using your talent, your intelligence, and your ability to make a sale and then get paid for it based upon your productivity and accomplishments!

"But before you do that on the scale we're talking about here, you've got to make some changes in yourself! You've got to have a positive attitude about yourself and other people. You've got to have a specific goal because if you don't have a destination, you can't get there! Before you can sell anything to anybody, you've got to make a friend of them because they have to trust you before they'll even think of buying from you! You've got to be able to create a need for your product that's so overwhelming they'll wonder how they were ever able to do without it! But most important of all, you have to create the kind of excitement and enthusiasm that accounts for the majority of the reasons people buy anything! Because believe me, excitement and enthusiasm are the most catching feelings in the world!

"Now you might say, 'I've been selling this product for years. How can I get excited or enthusiastic about something I'm bored with?' And I'm here to tell you that by the time you leave here today, you're going to be so motivated that you'll get excited and enthusiastic just thinking about being part of the traffic on the way home!"

As the room erupts in laughter he knows they belong to him. Each and every one. Totally. They will sit listening and scribbling madly in notepads to record his words for posterity with the heartfelt conviction that their very future depends on putting his ideas on paper. Interspersed throughout the day, he'll make reference to a book he's written or tapes (tape recorders are not allowed in the auditorium) that deal in depth with a specific subject and, of course, will be available for sale at the door. Before they leave, they will have spent an average of $175 to $230 on the seminar, on tapes they may view once, books which will probably gather dust on a shelf, and notes which will end up stuck in a drawer before eventually ending up in a trashcan.

The next day they'll bound off to work, anxious to put to use all their new and exciting attitudes and enthusiasm in quest of the brand-new goals they learned to formulate during the seminar.

The day after that, life will be back to normal. They won't even realize that what they heard—what was then so exciting, new, innovative, and motivating—was really nothing more than what they already knew and had been doing all along for the same results they were getting before attending the seminar.

Only the words were different.

The top producers who didn't have the time (or inclination) to attend the seminar will still be writing 90 percent of the business while those who did will remain among the 90 percent of the salespeople writing 10 percent of the business until the next incredible new seminar for instant success rolls around.

In the meantime, the sales trainers and motivators go their merry way, bouncing from one part of the country to another doing their thing.

So you ask, "Who are those masked men and women? Where did they learn all that stuff? And does it really work?"

Let's take a moment and look.

Almost anyone who has ever attended a seminar recognizes the man or woman described above. They are always physically attractive, dress in up-to-the-minute style, have a smooth, easy personality, are excellent public speakers, probably led their class in high school and college stage productions, and a pep rally could not have been pulled off without them.

Generally, sales trainers and motivators fall into one of two categories. They are either employed full-time by corporations or are freelancers who are self-employed, giving seminars for companies, associations, and organizations or to the general public, promoting their seminars through newspaper ads and salespeople calling on companies.

The Corporate Sales Trainer

This is typically a salaried position created for a man or woman who at one time was actually a salesperson for what is usually a high-turnover sales organization. Although there are definitely exceptions, these positions are generally occupied by people who were unable to make a living at sales.

Just before the general manager could show them what a termination form looked like on the way out, they were fortunate enough to have a friend "upstairs" intercede on their behalf. After all, they know the product inside out as well as the procedures and the paperwork involved in the sale. They know how prospecting is supposed to be done, the details of product knowledge, its variety of uses and applications. And what's more, they have actually been in the field.

Considering all the above, their function is important as long as it is restricted to the mechanics and procedures of the sale. They're also perfect for recruiting new salespeople as well as supervising them for an initial period to free up the sales manager for more important responsibilities.

Too often, unfortunately, their area of authority is far too broad, extending into actual selling techniques which they insist on passing on to trainees and in which they have personally demonstrated a lack of skill, knowledge, and/or experience; hence a field pro's first advice to a new salesperson is, "Forget everything you learned in training now that you're in the real world."

If you doubt this, consider for just a moment that no salesperson worth his or her income would consider taking a sales training position on a salaried basis. They are accustomed to making a much more substantial amount of money on straight commission, or salary-plus-commission.

On the other side of the coin, and unfortunately so, companies tend to mirror our nation's attitude toward education and training. Instead of recruiting top people with established track records of performance in a given field, to train others in the skills they have acquired and demonstrated, and paying them an income equal to or exceeding that which they could make in the field, companies almost always relegate training to a low-salaried position.

That's why skilled, experienced professionals would no more consider training than highly qualified people consider teaching when they can make so much more in the commercial and industrial marketplace with fewer headaches.

The Sales Motivator

Freelance sales motivators are first and foremost combination entertainers/public speakers whose talents lie almost exclusively in those areas. They generally have a smooth, practiced, and articulate presentation combined with a casual, easygoing, likable personality which extends their popularity on the circuit.

Including a wide variety of backgrounds ranging among ministers, doctors, attorneys, politicians, psychologists, sociologists, anthropologists, and every other "ologist" you can think of, all have two characteristics in common. First, they love being the center of attraction on stage, and second, although great at selling themselves to an audience, few have ever successfully sold a product or service for a living, other than their own books and tapes.

To cite an example, I attended a two-day seminar given by one of the most popular "gurus" on the real estate circuit. I will admit the hours literally flew as this person expounded to more than a hundred people the most effective selling methods, techniques, and attitudes absolutely necessary to achieve success in real estate. The information, stories, and personal experiences of the speaker were expertly woven in an absolutely entertaining presentation which could have been showcased on a Las Vegas stage.

Between anecdotes I watched people scribbling page after page of notes they could have gleaned from any basic selling primer.

But most disappointing was learning several weeks later that this person never had a real estate license and had never sold anything for a living—in fact, not even his own home!

Yet thousands of sales agents perpetuate their own mediocrity, basing their lives, incomes, and the future of their families on "the gospel" presented in seminars and books written by this so-called expert. When you get right down to it, it makes about as much sense as buying a book on "How to Reach the Heights of Passionate Orgasmic Love" written by someone who's never been able to get a date in his entire life!

But don't take me wrong. I'm not trying to imply that these folks do not perform an important function. A large number of those on the speaking circuit provide an outstanding contribution of information and techniques designed to improve and heighten the self-esteem and confidence of those in the audience who are willing to put their methods to use.

Contrary to popular belief, however, while those areas might contribute to the individual's self-image, they have little or nothing to do with increasing powers of persuasion. In that area most of the concepts are nothing more than the same timeworn tactics and techniques found in hundreds, maybe thousands of sales books written since the 1940s. Like those books, the sales motivators change the words, add humor to the examples, and present them with a slightly different slant, but in the end are all saying the same old things.

They are the gurus promoting and perpetuating the principles you will see in the next chapter, which, as applied to today's society, are nothing more than . . .

MYTHS!

2

EXPLODING THE MYTHS

Companies surviving today's economic and customer demands spend billions of dollars each year to purchase and continually upgrade sophisticated state-of-the-art equipment for increased efficiency, more cost-effective operations, and higher productivity and profitability. They recruit the most educated, qualified, and experienced people available for positions at all levels of management. Accounting functions once performed by armies of clerks and bookkeepers are now streamlined by computer systems. Engineering and production is handled more easily, efficiently, profitably, and quickly by computer-aided design and flow systems. Human resource departments, once referred to as "Personnel," are now staffed by highly trained specialists who are expert in dealing with employees and their variety of problems, both personal and professional, which relate to their jobs and subsequently to their efficiency and productivity. Marketing, advertising, and public relations departments, once concerned only with getting the product and company name in front of the consumer, today use highly sophisticated marketing demographics to present their product in the best possible light for the highest consumer acceptance, attraction, and demand.

Yet, in spite of these massive expenditures to keep up with technology, many companies continue to fall short of their goals during the last and most final step: the actual sale of their product to the end user. This is the point at which everything ultimately balances on the salesperson, that one individual the prospective customer sees who represents the company, employees, efforts, capital investment, and ultimately the final result on the profit or loss statement. All the technology, expertise, creativity, and capital investment is meaningless and wasted if that person is not completely trained to effectively deal with the prospect, especially if he or she is still using Stone Age persuasion techniques no longer acceptable—and in some cases even insulting—to the contemporary buying public.

Old-school methods, *if they ever really worked,* may have been effective years ago when the majority of people were uninformed, uneducated, and content to accept the modest lifestyle and desires of most Americans, which centered around a basic home, station wagon, 2.5 children, dog, and lifelong job with a moderate retirement at the end.

There may have existed that idyllic time when people cared about others more than themselves; when someone was persuaded to do something strictly for the benefit of the person requesting it; when someone was persuaded to buy something because the salesperson would "win the contest" or because "he is such a nice guy and oh sooooooo friendly."

If those days ever did exist, they are for the most part gone. Today, that glad-handing, backslapping good ol' boy with the run-down heels, the latest joke, and the martini-lunch expense account has been replaced by a professional, educated man or woman in a smart stylish business suit who is not there to backslap, tell funny stories, or buy lunch for the hell of it.

When they open a briefcase, slip a modem attachment into a telephone jack, and use a computer to access the latest information, YOU KNOW THEY'RE THERE TO DO BUSINESS! And in order to accomplish it properly, they must have special skills which range far beyond being likable or just having a warm, friendly, pleasant personality.

The Age of Specialization

Today we live in an age of specialization and a highly diverse, competitive, stressful, and demanding society. Primarily this is a result of the fact that there have been more changes in the last fifty years than in the entire recorded history of our planet.

In every industry and field, instant worldwide access to a constant flow of information and technology, continually revised and updated, reveals new and more efficient products, methods, approaches, services, and solutions to everyday situations.

As with any benefit, however, this carries with it responsibilities and requirements for specialized information and education, which more often than not contradict premises previously accepted as fact, thereby triggering a conflict with what we call human nature and its natural tendency of . . .

Resistance to Change

Most people are amenable to change when it comes to their style of dress or hair, scents, food, and the variety of products they use. After all, those things are personal to them. But when it comes to something which will have a direct bearing on their lives,

Average People Don't Like Change!

They are comfortable doing something the way it's always been done. For one, they don't have to take any chances on a nice, safe, no-risk method with predictable results. They don't have to take the time or make the effort to learn anything new.

If you have even the most basic knowledge of computers, for example, you are aware that software and hardware technology constantly changes to meet demands for greater efficiency, speed, and accuracy. In fact, many of the software programs designed for computers built as few as five years ago are completely incompatible with the hardware designed for today's operations. They simply can't keep pace anymore.

Yet there are a lot of people who will continue to use that old equipment and those old software programs until they fall apart and can't be replaced. Why? Because *resistance to change* is a natural inclination of the average person, regardless of the benefits. Using new, up-to-date technology would require effort, looking at the tasks to be performed from a different point of view. It would require throwing out old manuals to learn new methods and approaches compatible with today's standards and demands.

But to the majority of people, those we refer to as "average," even more efficient results aren't worth the effort involved in accepting change of any kind unless pressured by necessity.

It's almost like growing up. As a little boy you spend a lot of years learning the rules of acceptance by other little boys. Most of those are rough-and-tumble, in everything from greetings to games. Suddenly you discover girls! And you either accept very quickly that the rules are different or you find yourself left out in the cold. One way or another, the easy way or the hard way, you eventually learn to accept it.

Willingness to change, to have the determination that your attitudes and techniques are based upon the best and most current information available, is more critical to success than all other factors combined. Yet, a glance at corporate America confirms that resistance to an obvious era of change is one of the major problems in the United States today.

Sears, which pioneered catalogue sales, refused to accept the buying public's attitude and shift toward the use of major credit cards while their competitors, willing to innovate, captured the bulk of their market. By the time Sears accepted the facts, it was too late and they were forced to close the very division they had founded.

General Motors refused to accept the public shift to smaller automobiles. Since then, they have paid a heavy price and continue to do so with their back now against the wall.

IBM, refusing to acknowledge the personal computer as a major product for the consumer market in the early and mideighties, was overrun with competition. As a result, in 1993 they announced there would be no stockholder dividends for the first time in their history.

The same is true of the majority of people who specialize in persuasion for a living. Although they are generally high-performance people requiring specialized knowledge in the most critical aspect of their livelihood, the human mind, resistance to change still plays a detrimental role.

One is the individual, for example, who will disagree with and stubbornly refuse to listen to ideas, concepts, or approaches which are new and unfamiliar. He proclaims loudly that he knows everything there is to know about any given subject based upon his fifteen or twenty years' experience. Most often, however, this is the mark of the person who, instead of having twenty years' experience, really has only one year's experience twenty times.

That's why I have no doubt that this chapter may be read with some measure of surprise, disagreement, and even ridicule.

> *"Man's mind, stretched to a new idea, never goes back to its original dimensions."* —OLIVER WENDELL HOLMES

If you happen to be in sales, you might scan the following pages saying to yourself, "This guy is playing with a forty-card deck! He's refuting all the basics, all the things I've been taught since my first day in sales. If they don't work, how is it that I've been making a decent income with them?"

That would be perfectly natural. In fact, I said exactly the same thing. I learned those same basics, applied them, and was also fortunate enough to make a living. But I also noticed changes over the years. Selling was getting tougher. It was becoming more difficult to maintain consistency.

It was not until I started really looking at people that I experienced a miraculous realization:

People Will Always Be People.

Someone stuck in the old school rationalizes and defends their refusal to change because "People will always be people."

That's true, and because it is, it means that they are in a constant state of change!

Twenty-five years ago, people weren't afraid to leave their homes unlocked. Those few living on the street without visible means of support were picked up for vagrancy, not just labeled "homeless" and left to struggle and even die there. Metal detectors in airports were unheard of, and that we'd ever have them in elementary and high schools was beyond imagining! The auto mechanic's primary tools were sockets, wrenches, and screwdrivers. Today it's a multitude of computers, and the mechanic who refuses to advance with technology is now relegated to sweeping the garage floor.

Leave It to Beaver and *Father Knows Best* families don't exist anymore. Single parents account for a major portion of the population. Dual careers exist in 85 percent of families in the United States. Lifestyles and expectations are more demanding than they have ever been. And the name on the door of the president of the company is just as likely to start with Ms. as Mr.

People, their families, and the way they think and live continue to change, and their jobs and responsibilities become more time consuming. They are more educated, informed, sophisticated, and knowledgeable, with definite ideas of what they do and do not want and how they will accept or refuse to be treated. What all this boils down to is the result that today's consumers respond differently to buying products and services than consumers ten or even five years ago.

Realizing this, it should not have been difficult for me to understand that those who purchased from me were doing so for completely different reasons than the assumptions I had made, all of which were based upon old, out-of-date concepts. Once I finally discovered the real reasons, and applied a system of persuasion based upon those reasons to other clients, I was suddenly making a better living than I ever thought possible. In fact, my success ratio increased by at least two to one.

This chapter examines and disintegrates the rules of selling and persuasion which for more than thirty years have been preached, generalized, and exaggerated to the point that they no longer apply to contemporary attitudes—those same rules, unfortunately, to which most people and quite a few businesses still adhere, investing their futures, fortunes, and very livelihoods. Then they wonder why they fail.

They are the principles which today are accepted as gospel but which, in reality, are nothing more than . . .

MYTHS

MYTH #1: *In order to succeed, you must always have a positive mental attitude!*

FACT: More people have taken this trip to Fantasy Island and never returned than any other!

Positive mental attitude is the most beloved and promoted of all myths held sacred by the gurus. Unfortunately, the way it is promoted, it is also the most direct course to negativity, a poison which first turns you against other people and ultimately against yourself.

If you think this a contradiction, consider: You're with a client who has no money, no credit, and no interest in the product you have to sell. "PMA" dictates that there just has to be a way to turn this around.

"You can do it!" you tell yourself. "If you think you can, you can! Keep that positive attitude!" That's what all the books say, so it must be true. So you use one closing technique after another. You put every ounce of energy and positive thinking into it that you can muster. Unfortunately it doesn't work for you in that situation and to make matters worse, every client after that turns out to be the same.

How do you feel at the end of the day after doing your best to maintain your positive mental attitude, just knowing that somehow you should have been able to convince them, only to face the fact that you didn't? And what if the same thing happens tomorrow . . . and the next day . . . and the next?

The salesperson who gets up every morning saying, "I am definitely going to have a great day! I am going to make a sale today! I am! I am!" is simply setting him- or herself up for the possibility of wasting valuable time, energy and emotion, which results in disappointment and failure! This kind of strategy makes about as much sense as a poker player betting his entire stake on the next hand before seeing the cards. Regardless of how professional he is and his knowledge of the odds or even the people against whom he is playing, he cannot possibly expect to win until he at least sees the hand.

In a sales or persuasion situation it's even worse because the person who, based upon positive mental attitude, insists he or she is going to succeed without first knowing the subject's point of view, motivations, or ability to make a decision is betting something of far more value than money. He or she is betting confidence, ego, pride, and every ounce of emotion. That's when positive mental attitude becomes nothing more than a camouflage for desperation.

That's when PMA becomes *premeditated mental anguish.*

In the real world there are good days when everything goes right and bad days when everything seems to go wrong. To deny it is about as logical as running blindfolded across a freeway. The result will be the same. The more someone insists that he or she is going to have a good day and then doesn't, the faster the slide.

It begins with little more than anxiety, a tiny suspicion stealthily creeping into the back of your mind, which leads to doubt.

"Gee, I wonder if I'm doing something wrong? I'm doing my best to keep a positive mental attitude, but things don't seem to be working."

Still maintaining your PMA, you try even harder. "I am going to succeed at this! I have to!"

At this point, doubt has evolved into frustration and desperation, the only result of which will be mistakes, carelessness, and continued failure. Even if the odds were stacked in your favor, at this point and operating under this attitude, your chances for successful persuasion are little better than zero.

The next step is anger, first directed against your circumstances: "I can't believe I'm in this situation! I don't deserve this!" Then against others: "Those stupid people! They're idiots! Why can't they understand the simplest concept?" And ultimately against yourself: "I'm the one who's stupid. How many times do I have to fail before I smarten up and get it through my thick head that this isn't working? That maybe this job isn't for me?"

The last and final slip will send you plummeting into apathy. "The hell with it. Nothing's ever worked for me in the past, so why should this be different? I guess I just have to resign myself to it and accept what comes my way."

The idea of using a positive mental attitude in an attempt to convince yourself of favorable results is useless and self-defeating because your brain associates and evaluates subconsciously much faster than you can think at the conscious level. If it recognizes a negative situation, it registers immediately as such and no amount of "positive thinking" is going to change it. It's similar to driving to an intersection only to notice at the last second that the light is red. Do you have to think first about moving your right foot from the gas to the brake pedal and then about applying moderate pressure? If that were true, streets would be littered with wrecked vehicles. Instead, your brain instantly reacts by screaming, "STOP THE CAR!" a split second before your foot slams the brake pedal to the floor.

It's the same with positive thinking. To say to yourself, "I'm going to think positive about this," requires just that—thinking. But your brain has already processed the information and made a judgment long before the thought process could begin. At that point, thinking positive means, "I'm not going to think negatively about this," which makes as much sense as saying, "I'm not going to think of the color blue." You just have and will continue to do so each time you repeat what you are trying not to do!

Instead of trying to convince yourself that every day is going to be great, make the resolution that if you simply do the best job you can, using all the knowledge you've gained, you will either succeed in a given situation . . . or you won't. Either way you'll be ahead of the game because every challenge gives you a new experience from which to learn and the more you learn, the more you will eventually succeed. Not only are you then prepared to bounce back from the bad days without risking negativity, but you'll also be better prepared to take advantage of the days when things actually go your way.

MYTH #2: *You must have specific goals, write them down, read them at least three times a day, and STICK to them.*

FACT: Part B of the positive mental attitude program, this is another great way to make your life miserable.

The most common mistake people make in setting goals is doing so in areas completely out of their control. The shop owner who starts the day proclaiming that she is definitely going to sell a thousand dollars' worth of merchandise without knowing whether a customer will even walk through the door is setting herself up for incredible disappointment.

And even setting goals in areas you can control has pitfalls. If you set your goals so low that they are easily attainable, what's the point? You then settle for mediocrity or levels below even minimum standards of acceptability. Not exactly what you'd call an accomplishment.

If you set them too high and can't achieve them in the desired time frame, two things happen.

First, you start calling yourself a failure (one of the results of PMA) and second, you begin to plunge into an even deeper slump because the natural inclination is to push harder. And the harder you push, the worse it becomes.

For example, have you ever sat across a table or stood across the hood of a car from Mr. Warmth? He's that salesman who is personality personified. Everything about him tells you he's going to be your best buddy, *like it or not!* As the conversation progresses, you indicate that you'll probably end up purchasing something, but you want to look around. Suddenly Mr. Warmth begins a slow, methodical transformation into something resembling the character in *An American Werewolf in London*. The eyes narrow and his bright shiny smile suddenly gleams with menacing teeth as he begins to get nastier by the minute.

This is your typical goal-oriented salesman who isn't doing too well for the month and may even be in a slump. The harder he pushes, the farther you back off. The more you back off, the harder he pushes, until he becomes so rude you wouldn't buy anything from this guy if he chipped in for half.

Hence the saying "The harder I try the behinder I get."

Now, let's say you set your goals so that you have to exert yourself to achieve them. Once you've accomplished that, what's the next step? A higher goal, of course. And a higher goal after that, and after that, and after that and so on until your whole life is nothing but one big goal. When you achieve it, life is great. When you don't you're back to being a failure again, teetering on the edge of negativity.

Yet another pitfall of specific goal setting occurs when you have an extraordinary streak. Suddenly you get into that "slot" (everyone has been there at one time or another) when you have the fabled Midas touch. You can do absolutely no wrong! You sell when you would have bet there wasn't a chance! The next thing you know, you're halfway through the time period and have already achieved more than the specific goal you set. Now what happens? You know as well as I. This is when specific goal setting actually causes complacency. The normal tendency, whether conscious or unconscious, is to sit back and relax because you've already reached the goal! Unfortunately, this will usually initiate the start of your next slump.

It shouldn't surprise you to learn that people who have achieved outstanding success never selected it as a specific goal to be reached within a certain time frame. In fact, you've seen and heard hundreds of examples to the contrary.

"I never in a million years ever imagined receiving this award. To be truthful, it comes as a complete surprise and all I can say is thank you to the people who believed in and supported me," is a common statement made by actors, athletes, entertainers, scientists, and other people who have achieved notoriety and recognition as the best in their field.

When Jim Courier, Andre Agassi, Pete Sampras, and Monica Seles were interviewed after winning their respective number-one ranking as world champions in tennis, each stated that they never set that position as a specific goal. Instead, they decided long before reaching first place that whether they ranked number one or number fifty their main goal was always to play the absolute best game they could each and every day while learning and having as much fun as possible.

The person who says "I'm going to be happy when I finally make a hundred thousand dollars!" has already committed himself to being miserable, absolutely refusing to accept happiness until he reaches a goal, forgoing enjoyment along the way. While he's eating breakfast, he's planning what he's going to have for lunch. When he's eating lunch, he's looking forward to dinner. And after dinner, he's forgotten what he had the two previous meals because he never had the opportunity to enjoy them.

Wouldn't it be a shame if you came to the end of the road and someone said, "Wow, you lived in a great era and a wonderful country. What were some of the most beautiful, memorable moments in your life?" and all you could describe was the goals you accomplished?

Did you ever know someone who was so intent on reaching their destination that they never got to enjoy the trip? Almost like driving from Los Angeles to Miami. There's some gorgeous scenery between those two cities. Some of it is even worth stopping to look at and enjoy.

Just like your life.

Based upon personal experience, I can tell you that if all you allow yourself to concentrate on is attaining a specific goal without having a lot of fun thrown in for good measure, you'll never be happy, *even when you reach the goal!* The attainment of a goal is nothing more than the successful completion of a series of steps toward that goal. If you designate each of the steps as an enjoyable progression to the goal, not only will you attain it, you will also have fun in the process.

On the other hand, if you find that you're taking yourself so seriously that you can't have fun in what you do, get away from it and find something else.

One of the oldest sayings is that life is what's happening to you while you're making other plans. So why not enjoy it? Isn't that really what life is all about? Getting as much enjoyment as possible from every day, every person you meet, doing the best job you can in every situation, and learning as much from your losses as you do from your wins?

If you do, you may just find yourself having more fun and going further than any goal you ever dreamed possible.

MYTH #3: *In order to succeed you must look successful.*

FACT: "Appearances can be deceiving" and "You can't judge a book by its cover."

At the end of a flight from Chicago to Los Angeles I was in a long, slow line of people filing off the plane. As we approached several crew members standing near the exit, the lady in front of me said, "Please tell the pilot that was one of the smoothest landings I've ever experienced. In fact, I hardly felt the wheels touch." Whereupon the shortest woman of the uniformed crew said, "Thank you, ma'am. I am the pilot."

Somewhat embarrassed, the lady giggled and said, "Oh, my goodness! I never would have guessed."

"And why is that, ma'am?" the woman pilot asked.

Hesitating, the lady responded, "Uh, well, because you're so, uh, uh, well, you're a woman and you're also shorter than I would have imagined, I guess."

Smiling, the pilot leaned toward her and in a low, courteous voice said, "Ma'am, I just fly the plane. I don't carry it on my back."

Whether you're a manager, salesperson, client, or negotiator, assuming anything about the person sitting across from you at the table based solely upon their appearance can be deadly!

The television series *Columbo* best illustrated this. What appeared to be a bumbling, klutzy detective in a disheveled trench coat shuffled his way through a variety of cases. Combining his style of dress with a deceptively slow-witted, casual manner of almost nonsensical questioning, he invariably put the prime suspect at ease. Then, just as he was about to leave, he'd stop, turn around, and say something like, "Oh, see how stupid I am, I almost forgot to ask you . . ." The zinger! Because by that time, the suspect was so overconfident that he was caught totally off guard and usually let slip some piece of information which would eventually be used to nail him as the guilty one.

Just a TV show? Not really. There are plenty of Columbos out there who use exactly the same technique with precision marksmanship.

This myth fails to consider that the importance of dress and general appearance depends almost entirely on what you're trying to persuade someone of, who they are, and the setting. That's why it never ceases to amaze me how some companies associate the word "professionalism" with designer suits, ties, shirts, and shoes, when often just the opposite is true. In fact, overdressing can be less acceptable than underdressing, depending on the circumstances.

For example, the person across the table from me looks like he just stepped off the pages of *Gentleman's Quarterly*. Everything about him is styled, manicured, buffed, and polished, from the Rolex watch and gold diamond-studded cuff links to the Gucci shoes. His presentation is practiced, smooth, and articulate right down to the syllable. He hits all the right buttons and has all the right answers without even a moment's hesitation. If I'm looking for someone to represent me in a trial, I'd hire him in a minute. On the other hand, if he was trying to sell me a brand-new financial package or involve me in a limited partnership, I would be extremely cautious. This guy might just be a little too smooth, or, better put, a little too slick.

On the other side of the coin, one of the most professional and successful real estate salespeople I've ever known never wears a tie.

He espouses the theory that when people shop for a home, they dress in casual, comfortable clothing. When they meet him, dressed similarly, they are immediately put at ease, enabling him to pinpoint exactly what they want and can afford, and they are more open to what he has to sell.

Another good salesperson was up in his years, a widower and about half blind. Having no wife to oversee what he wore, his entrance every day was a humorous surprise. Yet, he was still on top of the sales list every month, selling even the most unlikely prospects.

By the way, did I mention he was almost blind? That's the clue. Since he couldn't see all that well, Ted was a better *listener* than anyone I ever knew, but more about that later.

In short, dressing professionally and for success is really nothing more than dressing to meet the expectations of the person sitting across the table from you to make them comfortable, open, and confident.

MYTH #4: *Enthusiasm is 60 percent of the sale.*

FACT: Show me a dentist who tells me, *with enthusiasm,* that he is looking forward to doing a root canal on me and I'll show you a patient leaving the office to find a new dentist with the speed of an Olympic sprinter!

You can have all the enthusiasm in the world, but if you're trying to persuade someone who has a totally closed and prejudiced mind, it won't do you a bit of good if you don't know the secrets to opening that mind.

You can have all the enthusiasm in the world, but if you're trying to persuade someone who has no interest in your product or idea, no use for it, or simply can't afford it, you still have nothing!

You can have all the enthusiasm in the world, but without knowledge, it's like a runaway horse racing without direction or destination. If you can't intelligently and confidently answer questions about your point of view, you cannot possibly persuade anyone of anything.

You can have all the enthusiasm in the world, but if you're not *professional* enough to know what to look for, how to listen to what someone is saying, and how to ask questions, you might just as well be Sad Sack. The result will be the same.

You can have all the enthusiasm in the world, but if you are not driven by the desire to be successful and the willingness to take the necessary action to accomplish that success, you might as well stay in bed.

During a 1993 football playoff game, the Houston Oilers literally walked down the field to accumulate thirty-five points against the Buffalo Bills' three points by halftime. After the game, Buffalo's quarterback revealed that in the locker room during halftime no one even mentioned the possibility of winning, and there was certainly no "enthusiasm" on the part of the players to start the second half, already down by thirty-two points. The only decision upon which the entire team agreed was to approach the remaining half as professionals, *one play at a time and giving it their very best!* Using that strategy, they tied the Oilers at thirty-eight points by the end of the fourth quarter, and ended up winning by a field goal in overtime, setting an NFL comeback record.

The Enthusiasm Catchall

Some managers, trainers, and motivators cite enthusiasm as the reason new salespeople frequently do well, and nothing could be farther from the truth. Instead, since they are not as well versed in product knowledge as some of the old pros, they attempt to stay out of trouble by asking questions and listening more than talking, thereby following the old adage, "Better to remain silent and thought a fool than open your mouth and remove all doubt."

Not knowing enough to educate their prospects in the intricacies of what they are selling, they end up giving them the perfect opportunity to talk about the subject they most prefer (themselves) and then buy something!

Enthusiasm has nothing to do with their success, and in fact the word itself is nebulous at best. Being "bouncy and bubbly" (as we have so often heard), trying to come off as excited, or sounding like a carny pitchman might be considered enthusiastic by one person, while another might label you as ready for the funny farm, where a white jacket with buckles on the sleeves is a fashion statement, or if not that extreme, just plain phony. Because enthusiasm means different things to different people.

One of the best examples is the Publishers' Clearing House commercials showing the van pulling up in front of someone's house to deliver their ten-million-dollar oversized check. While one lucky recipient launches into near hysterics, another responds with a slight smile and says, "Yup, sure excites me," and you know that's about as enthusiastic as this guy gets.

Too many people attempt to meet someone else's definition of enthusiasm. Invariably the result is a phony, insincere façade which is completely contrary to their personality, stands out like brown shoes at a black-tie affair, and causes immediate mistrust on the part of the person to whom they are talking. It can also be misinterpreted as a cover-up or compensation for lack of ability or just plain desperation trying to make a point.

As you will see in the following chapter, there are extremely efficient methods to accurately gauge the person across from you, then adjust your personality to theirs without compromising yourself.

MYTH #5: *The customer is the most important person in your life because he/she writes your paycheck.*

FACT: One of the worst statements to ever come down the pike, this is responsible for tags like "peddler," "hustler," and "just" a salesperson.

It may be of interest to you that if you are one of the 10 percent of the people who do 90 percent of the business as discussed earlier, you are in the top 5 percent income category in the entire United States. In fact, you are earning more than 95 percent of the entire population, including attorneys, physicians, and top-level executives.

You are a top producer aware of your value and conduct yourself accordingly. In short, you take a back seat, abuse, and discourtesy from *no one,* including customers, prospects, or even supervisors, who are usually intelligent enough to appreciate you as being in one of the few professions whose productivity can be precisely measured, and you are remunerated in amounts commensurate to that productivity. Under no circumstances can you effectively or consistently convince anyone of anything if you believe, and thus project the belief, that you are subordinate or subservient to them.

Instead, you are a professional providing a product, service, or idea that is valuable, and your time doing so is just as important as the time clients spend listening to you. Only by fostering and nurturing that attitude can you be consistently successful.

MYTH #6: *In order to persuade anyone to do or purchase anything, you must first make them your friend to establish trust and confidence in both you and your company.*

FACT: If you really believe this, you're putting your ego in front of your wallet.

Yet, this myth is so popular that a large real estate firm is running television commercials based upon the theme, "People don't care how much we know. They care how much we care."

While this cute little play on words may sound good and give you all the warm, fuzzy feelings intended by the creative team at the advertising agency, in the real world it's nothing more than mythological hogwash! People spending hundreds of thousands of dollars on a real estate investment demand the confidence of knowing that their money and interests are represented by a competent, knowledgeable professional with a track record of success, not merely someone who, while warm, caring, and friendly, doesn't know the business.

As is the case with most myths, this one is also based on fact—that in order to persuade, it is necessary to establish rapport. Where it falls apart is the assumption that establishing rapport is synonymous with "making friends."

In a sales situation, this is supposedly accomplished during a "warm-up" period with techniques which include everything from finding something (anything!) on which to compliment the subject, to conducting "small talk" in what is often a desperate search for common areas of interest, beliefs, etc., etc. And this is where it becomes a myth.

People in today's society are selective when it comes to making friends and the process is not taken lightly, nor is it accomplished in a matter of minutes. This is primarily due to a prevailing attitude of distrust fostered and solidified by awareness of current events and people's own experiences and associations. Everyone has had confidences broken by "friends" and/or coworkers they trusted. They are made aware daily by the news media that they can't trust politicians, their police departments, their kids' teachers, day-care center operators, or even, for that matter, their clergyman. In fact, when Clinton voters in the 1992 presidential election were surveyed, it was discovered that 48 percent said that although they voted for him, they did not trust him.

Yet, according to this myth, people are supposed to make friends with and trust the perfect stranger sitting before them making small talk, knowing full well that the salesperson's job, income, and livelihood are based on the ability to turn that small talk into a sales presentation and then to turn that presentation into an opportunity which usually involves taking money out of their pocket.

This naiveté goes back to beliefs fostered during the days of the backslapping salesman who was everybody's buddy. If it did work then, those days are over. In fact, perpetuating small talk in order to make friends today usually generates *mistrust* on the part of the person sitting across the table. In their minds they're saying, "When do we get to the point here? Why is he or she avoiding the issue?" They know you're there to persuade them of something and so do you. So who's kidding whom?

If, during the course of conversation, you have been able to discover the motivation which drives an individual's decision-making process and then effectively apply the benefits of your concept or product to those motivations, their level of trust in you or your company is irrelevant, unless, of course, you have said something either verbally or subliminally to make them *distrust* you, which is an altogether different problem which will be discussed in depth later.

At this point their only concern becomes the *assurance of protection* they will have once the decision process is concluded.

The Sears Roebuck empire was built on this concept. They didn't depend on their salespeople to spend time making friends, explaining how Sears does business with multiple stores throughout the nation and the world or showing financial statements. Instead, they demanded that their salespeople be courteous, attentive, and knowledgeable; inventoried what they knew people wanted to purchase; priced the stock based on its quality; and completed the decision-making process with their motto, "Satisfaction guaranteed or your money back!", giving their customers the *maximum assurance of protection.*

Rapport is crucial to persuasion in assisting you to accurately pinpoint motivators and satisfiers, described in the next chapter, and as you will see, there are extremely effective ways to accomplish it. Warm-ups, small talk, and "making friends" are not even a remote consideration.

MYTH #7: *You should always "be yourself" in a persuasion situation.*

FACT: If you are always "yourself," you're going to alienate people right and left.

Who are you? Really.

Do you act, think, and respond to people at a funeral the same as you would at a football game? Would you attempt to communicate with someone who is skeptical or cynical the same as you would a person who is open and accepting?

What if, by nature, you tend to be sarcastic and caustic? Would you be that way while trying to persuade someone of something?

Everyone has a multifaceted personality to adapt to different circumstances, people, and environments. If you maintain a specific and distinct personality, regardless of the personality and temperament of the person to whom you are presenting a point of view, your ability to communicate will be severely limited, as will your success.

The key to effective communication and persuasion is being able to understand the other person's point of view and the driving force behind their decision-making processes. In order to accomplish that effectively, your personality must be adaptable to theirs. This aspect of persuasion is both so critical and extensive that it will be covered in detail in several chapters of this book.

MYTH #8: *A smooth presentation is the key to persuasion.*

FACT: What you consider a smooth presentation and what the person to whom you are giving it considers a smooth presentation are usually entirely different.

If a presentation of any kind is so smooth that it leaves little or no room for questions, feedback, or responses, it is about as effective as a one-sided conversation, which quickly becomes boring. Additionally, a presentation can be so smooth and too good to be true that the listener becomes suspicious to the point that he or she begins to concentrate more on looking for holes than listening.

An effective presentation always leaves room for questions,

the answers to which show the subject beyond any doubt how the product, service, or idea can be customized to them, their point of view, and their specific motivators and satisfiers.

MYTH #9: *In order to establish credibility, you must have documentation to prove that everything you are saying is true.*

FACT: If you document everything, you are essentially saying, "I know you don't believe me so I'm going to prove it."

This has a threefold result: it bores the subject to tears, breaks down rapport, and makes him or her wonder what you're really trying to hide if you have to prove everything you say.

On the other hand, if you feel you need documentation because you're being questioned on every point, you obviously have not established rapport and will never persuade this person regardless of the documentation you produce.

MYTH #10: *In order to persuade someone of anything, you must create the need for that product, service, or idea.*

FACT: People don't buy needs, they buy wants!

Creating the need is another of the oldest and most misstated of all the myths.

If a business or personal relationship is heading for the tubes, try telling the other person that he or she *needs* you and see what response you trigger. They won't buy it. In fact, they'll actually go out of their way to prove just how much they *don't* need you!

Aside from products designed for basic survival, people think about and delay purchasing needs. They will, however, consistently buy wants, then justify that purchase by rationalizing a need for it!

From a very early age, everyone quite normally develops an aversion to needs. Their mothers told them they *needed* to eat their vegetables. If they didn't like milk, they were told they had to drink it because they *needed* the calcium that milk provides. They even *needed* to do the dishes and take out the garbage. They had to go to school because to make it in this world, you *need* an education.

Everyone likes to think that someone else needs them or their idea and then proceeds to emphasize that need or, worse yet, tries to create the need even if it doesn't exist. Why? Because the gurus have been telling us for years that's how it's done.

But what about the person who staunchly refuses to budge? He knows he doesn't need it and in truth, so do you. Do you keep pushing the need, trying to find any possible angle to make the point? That's like the salesperson with the fangs. The harder he pushes, the harder you push back. Yet most people do exactly that, wasting time and energy, and still end up not only losing the sale but causing antagonism on the part of their subject because they're approaching the problem from the wrong side.

Let's face it, if people based purchases strictly on needs, they wouldn't be collecting credit cards in stacks or going into hock up to their eyeballs. You may even know some of the people I'm talking about. Maybe even *intimately!* Sure, everyone needs transportation, but does anyone *need* a Jaguar, Cadillac, or Mercedes, just to go from point A to point B? They need shelter, but do they *need* a five-hundred-thousand-dollar home with a mortgage they can barely afford? Before they purchased it, they *wanted* that home. Afterwards, they will go to great lengths to explain exactly why they needed it.

You don't persuade anyone to do anything because they *need* to do it. But as you'll see, once you find the driving force behind their decision-making processes, make them *want* something intensely, and simply help them find and then rationalize a *need* for it, they'll purchase it regardless of its value and often even its affordability!

MYTH #11: *You've got to create excitement!*

FACT: What's exciting to one person may not be to another.

This myth perpetuates the old timeworn saying "Sell the sizzle, not the steak." Unfortunately, it is too general and does not address the differences in people. Here again, what's sizzling to one person might be really boring to another. But aside from that, what happens if you spend an entire discussion describing how exciting your product or idea is, only to have the subject tell you that excitement is the last thing they want?

Like enthusiasm, before you go creating excitement, you'd better find out exactly what it is the person sitting in front of you wants, which, by the way, is one of the easiest things to discover.

MYTH #12: *The most important aspect of persuasion is showing someone they have a problem and presenting a solution.*

FACT: If someone tells you they have a problem, that's one thing. If you tell them, you'll very quickly be the one with the problem.

In the real world, most people don't like to face or even admit to problems, much less be reminded of them by a total stranger. At best, if they do admit to one, they will tend to minimize it. Want to alienate someone really fast? Just keep harping on that problem they don't want to face.

On the other hand, if your purpose is to get them to listen to you, find out what is important to them and focus your conversation in the same context.

MYTH #13: *You must never prequalify someone's ability to accept you, your ideas, or product.*

FACT: Another spin-off from the old PMA myth, this one wastes time, energy, and emotion.

It's a given that you never know when there is the chance that your methods of persuasion will eventually work, that you may just strike the right chord to bring someone around to your way of thinking. But you definitely know when you *don't* have a chance. If the person sitting in front of you is blatantly closed-minded and refuses to listen or even consider what you have to say, you'd be better off talking to your dog. At least he'll look at you and maybe even respond.

If you know your client is without the emotional, financial, or decision-making capability to accept your idea, you are wasting valuable time, energy, and emotion beating a dead horse and, worse than that, dragging yourself down in the process.

Let go, attempt to learn something from the experience, and move on to the next one.

MYTH #14: *Before getting into the actual presentation, you must make your prospect commit to giving you a yes or no decision when you reach the end of it.*

FACT: This is another great myth which serves only to alienate people even before you have the chance to establish rapport.

In sales, this technique is called "boxing the prospect" or the timeworn "If I could, would you?" technique. Nowhere in the entire selling field is this more overused than in the vacation ownership industry, where there's an even more descriptive term for it, "breaking the pact." Those folks know that people who go to time-share presentations for a gift or a supposedly free vacation usually realize they're in for some very hard-sell techniques, usually from a so-called manager the salesperson calls in at the end who is really nothing more than a hard-hitting closer. As a result, before they arrive, the prospects often agree (make a pact) that absolutely nothing is going to convince any of them to purchase at the presentation.

Breaking that pact is the salesperson's job. "If I could show you something that would be of interest to you and is affordable, would you be prepared to purchase it?" Or "Other than the price, which I haven't discussed yet, is this something you feel you'd like to get involved in today?"

This practice is nothing more than a chapter from the guru gospel which preaches that you must take complete control in a selling situation, that the more commitments you get during the presentation, the more difficult it is for the prospect to back out without embarrassment. This may have worked long ago with some weak-willed people, but quite frankly, there aren't that many of those around anymore, and those who are don't have any money left. Attempting to take control of, "box," or force a commitment cannot be accomplished with contemporary prospects and in fact is more likely to create antagonism.

The biggest fallacy is that the control issue, like most of the myths, fails to take into account the other person's point of view. If you have agreed to listen open-mindedly to someone else's opinion, or to see their presentation of a product or concept, why in the world should you make any commitment before being presented the complete picture?

You shouldn't, and if they insist, they're simply forcing one of two reactions. You can tell them you would just as soon end the conversation here and now (which I would), or you may simply agree to those terms but mentally withdraw your original commitment to have an open mind. In either situation, rapport has definitely been damaged, if not altogether lost.

MYTH #15: *You've got to make sure that your presentation is so complete that it answers objections before they arise.*

FACT: People take action based upon acceptable answers to their questions or objections.

This myth limits the presentation to one-way communication and fails to take into account that most persuasion is finalized not based upon the presentation itself but rather on answers to the questions given in such a manner as to solidify a decision.

In fact, guiding a presentation based upon this myth actually removes the subject's reason to buy or agree!

Effective persuasion is **two-way communication** which both parties can understand, upon which they agree, and which causes the subject to take action. Allowing room for questions and even objections to which there are logical answers actually accelerates the entire persuasion process.

MYTH #16: *Avoid putting the subject in the position of having to give you a definite no at the end of your presentation. That gives you an open door to call back for a future possibility.*

FACT: This myth wastes your time and effort, and leads only to self-deception.

Most people are by nature nonconfrontational. They feel that giving a definite no to someone with whom they have established a decent rapport would be insulting, hurt his or her feelings, or require a defense of their position. To avoid these alternatives, they usually come up with "I want to think about it," or "I really have to talk with someone else before I do anything." What they are really saying is they are not buying the product or idea from you—ever!—but don't have the heart to come out and tell you.

Why this should be a surprise is anyone's guess. Who cannot remember one or both parents saying, "Let me think about

it," "I'll have to talk to your father (or mother)," or the equivalent, "We'll see," in response to an unusual or untimely request.

For that matter, you may have recently used it on your kids.
Because it works! Once that response is given, most people prefer to let the situation remain in limbo. Accepting it is simply
a way to avoid confronting the subject's real objection and at
the same time affords what they would like to believe is the luxury of hope. Unfortunately, that luxury is most often nothing
more than fantasy.

By encouraging the subject to express the real and specific
objection, you have an opportunity to either answer or overcome it. If the objection is valid and for one reason or another
insurmountable, it is far better to accept reality and go on to
the next topic. If it is not valid, you have another direction for
added persuasion.

MYTH #17: *If you lose a sale or fail to persuade someone,
forget it and go on to the next.*

FACT: Follow this myth and you'll feel like the robot walking
into a wall over and over, making the same mistakes continuously.

Losing a persuasion situation can be much more valuable than
winning one. If you haven't already guessed why, the one you
accomplished successfully is just that—one situation. The one
you lose and learn from will give you multiple achievements in
the future.

MYTH #18: *If you love helping and working with people, can make friends easily and establish trust, you're certain to be a success in sales!*

FACT: If you love helping and working with people and want to make new friends, get a job as a volunteer with the Salvation Army because you won't last long in sales.

There are thousands of people over the years who, hearing this myth, said, "Great! That's me!" and decided to launch their career in sales. Unfortunately, a large percentage of them ended up not only leaving the profession but leaving it as irreversible cynics with a general distaste for people.

What they failed to realize before making their career move is that people act, think, and respond differently to a salesperson than they do in a social situation.

That nice man you know in the church choir might be the sweetest, most down-to-earth human being you've ever met, willing to give his time and even money to anyone in need. He's so kind, generous, and sincere that it would be impossible to picture him any other way. Put him in front of a salesperson and you may see an entirely different picture. That sweet, kind-hearted, and generous soul may well turn into the most stubborn, closed-minded, irrational individual you've ever met, who hasn't the slightest twinge of guilt at lying through his teeth. He may tell you one thing one minute, and the very next contradict himself. If confronted, he'll deny he ever said anything in the first place. He may lead you down the merry path, letting you think there's some real interest, and at the very end not think twice about wasting your time or your money.

Why? Because, after all, you're "just" a salesperson. That's your job, isn't it?

This should not be a surprise. When people are in front of a salesperson, they're often at their very worst. In many cases they're uncomfortable, defensive, and just plain scared because they know that person's job is to take money out of their pocket if at all possible.

Realizing what you're dealing with, understanding things from their point of view, and being a true professional is the only salvation you have. Liking or loving people has nothing whatever to do with success in dealing with them and in fact may be a handicap.

MYTH #19: *Selling and persuasion are a process of closing objections. There are specific "closes" for every objection, and you can expect to use at least five different closes to get the sale. To be effective, you must know which to use, when, and how to use them to push people into a decision.*

FACT: If you haven't properly implemented the persuasion process, no amount of "closing" will change a negative decision to a positive one and, in fact, usually only serves to further alienate your subject.

In the old days, it was said that "a prospect is a prospect until he buys or dies." This was the point at which the professional closer really got to show his stuff by hammering the subject with one close after another until either the closer or the prospect eventually broke down.

The list of closes to specific objections was as long as your arm, including, to name just a few, the box close, open end close, final objection close, if-I-could/would-you close, summary close, sympathy close, budget close, sales contest close, promise close, and, yes, we must not forget the old standby, the Ben Franklin close, none of which merit explanation or have any place in sales today. They go back to an era when a signed contract was a final contract. The prospect became a customer, the salesperson received the commission, and it was a done deal.

Then something happened to change all this: the customer's right to recision. It was a law passed in nearly every state which specified that regardless of the amount of money the customer puts down or the legal forms, contracts, and paperwork he or she signs, that customer may have anywhere from three to ten days (depending on the state) to reconsider the purchase, back out of the deal, and receive a 100 percent refund.

Ignoring this, the gurus are still teaching the techniques of those timeworn closes, salespeople are spending hours wearing down or outright insulting clients, and recision percentages are skyrocketing once the customers escape their clutches, leaving the salesperson still thinking he's accomplished a coup, expecting a commission check which will never arrive.

The fact is, those people were not truly persuaded of anything. They simply did what any of us might do in a similar situation with a person who is so obnoxious you can barely wait to get away from him.

For example, have you ever been in the middle of a heated discussion with someone who kept insisting on their point of view, barely listening to what you had to say? What did you finally do? Chances are, you simply agreed with them to put an end to it. But did they really make their point? Were you really persuaded of anything? Hardly! And if they did get you to agree temporarily, was there anything to prevent you from changing your mind?

The days of browbeating someone into agreement are over. True persuasion is a science and anyone attempting to persuade can no longer be a phony, backslapper, or bully. And although salespeople who are still using those methods complain vociferously about recision laws, federal and state regulations are cleaning up entire industries, demanding professional techniques, knowledge, and people.

Once persuasion is successfully accomplished, the only "closing" necessary is overcoming the natural tendency of people to procrastinate, to avoid making a decision even after they know they want something. This is when the "I want to think about it," or "I never make a decision without thinking it over for a few days" objection comes into play. When this happens, the subject is telling you one of two things: that you have not done an adequate job of making him want to make a decision or that he is not financially or otherwise capable of taking action.

If the first is correct, you simply misread or did not place enough emphasis on that person's motivational triggers, which will be discussed thoroughly in the next chapter. If, however, the problem is truly financial, no amount of hammering or browbeating will change things. The only technique which may turn a decision to your favor at this point is a "takeaway."

"If you like the idea and see how it fits your situation, then the only thing really left to think about is affordability. And as much as I hate to say it, I think we can agree that if it's not affordable, all the thinking in the world won't change that, so maybe this just isn't for you and there's no harm in saying so."

This close has been responsible for hundreds of thousands of commission dollars and is effective because it accomplishes a twofold result. First, if the person truly can't afford it, they will generally come out and say so, allowing you to courteously end the presentation right then and there, avoiding the unnecessary waste of time in follow-up calls. On the other hand, if he can afford it but wants to procrastinate, it's usually because he doesn't want to be pushed into buying something from a salesperson anxious to sell. This technique "pulls" him into the decision.

As a simple experiment, try to make a child play with a toy he likes but is not particularly interested in at the time. You can push it toward him all day and he will refuse to play with it. However, take it away and in full view give it to another child and see what happens.

Skillful persuasion does not entail multiple closes to an endless number of objections. It simply requires listening to your subject, comprehending what they are really saying, and finally, applying specialized techniques and knowledge.

MYTH #20: *Everyone likes a winner!*

FACT: Winners seldom rank high in popularity contests among those who don't share in their productivity.

Winners are typically solitary, unwilling to participate in the day-to-day conversations and gossip discussed at length by "average" people. As a result, although their coworkers usually have a certain degree of respect for them, few if any like them and instead tend to congregate and commiserate among themselves, looking at winners with envy and even antagonism.

"He got lucky again." "Isn't it strange that she always seems to be at the right place at the right time?" "He has an inside track." "She has pull in the corner office." These are just a few of the reasons to which average people attribute the success of high-performance producers. In reality, those "reasons" are nothing more than rationalizations to justify their own mediocrity and a desperate search to find as many people as possible to agree with them. It makes them all feel better about themselves, excusing, at least on the surface, their own deficiencies.

This practice exists in organizations both large and small and, although common to human nature, is another form of negativity. As such, it is dangerously insidious and will spread with the speed of cancer to affect the performance of everyone except the winners, since popularity is seldom high on their list of priorities anyway.

MYTH#21: Everyone deserves to be successful!

FACT: All men are created equal—a few are just more equal than the rest.

It would be great if everyone in the world could just sit back and get what they deserved. On second thought, maybe not everyone. With a few exceptions we could probably all offer, people in the real world usually deserve the success they achieve and earn it based upon their desire and willingness to take action and, in most cases, to sacrifice.

While some are satisfied sitting around doing the same old things day after day, there will always be those special few, that 10 percent referred to time and again in this book, who constantly strive to learn, improve, and grow in the commitment to themselves and in attaining whatever it is that they want in life.

They are truly the people who deserve success.

There you have them, the myths which for years have been expounded upon in books, tapes, and seminars as formulas for instant success and wealth but have, in reality, been detrimental to many who believed and followed them with inflexible and religious fervor.

Truly successful people realize that their success is based upon the ability to effectively communicate with changing people in a changing world; the open-mindedness to accept that what yesterday called controversial, today describes as technology; and the willingness to put knowledge to use for themselves, to try something different to succeed, to be more effective with . . .

SUBLIMINAL PERSUASION

3

SUBLIMINAL PERSUASION

Your ability to effectively persuade, as well as the direction in which you are persuaded, literally determines the course of your future every day of your life.

For example, it can mean the difference between being employed or unemployed, making two hundred fifty thousand dollars or twenty thousand per year, and enjoying the luxury that life has to offer or constantly worrying about paying bills. But far more important than financial considerations, it also dictates the quality of your life.

Will you be able to establish relationships with those you choose, or accept what comes along? Will those relationships be happy and fulfilling, or stressful, unrewarding, and emotionally devastating? Will you be able to design the direction of your life, or drift randomly from one circumstance to another?

The ability of others to persuade you also plays a determining role. The profession or job you select, where you live,
how you raise and educate your children, and what products
you buy all depend on how you are persuaded and its subsequent impact on your life.

Considering its importance, few people really know what
persuasion is, much less the intricacies involved in its effective
application.

A Communications Process

Persuasion is first and foremost a process of bidirectional communication during which one individual or group of individuals convinces another individual or group of individuals to
adopt their theories, ideas, or beliefs as factual. Professional
persuasion, as it applies to selling yourself, an idea, opinion,
or product, goes one step further. Not only does it include
your ability to convince people, but, of equal importance,
your ability to stimulate them to take action based upon that
decision.

The first word to stress in the definition is *bidirectional*. Before you can even begin to persuade anyone of anything, you
must first have a very thorough understanding of their point of
view, desires, aspirations, and motivations. In a selling situation, salespeople too often refer to that part of the presentation
as the "warm-up," the goal of which is to learn something
about the prospect and in the course of conversation to make
that person "a friend."

As we saw in the myths, the tactic contributes very little and may even be detrimental to this most critical part of the persuasion process.

Whether you happen to be in a superior's office attempting to get approval on an idea or project or in front of a prospect to whom you want to sell a product, the fact of the matter is you both know exactly why you're there. Both of you also know that the friendly conversation you're conducting is nothing more than an attempt on your part to set the stage or, in some cases, a reluctance to get to the point, the only result of which is to make both people very uncomfortable.

While this might once have been somewhat tolerated or acceptable, people today want to cut to the chase and get down to business. If out of simple courtesy they do participate in so-called pleasant conversation, what they actually say at this point is only a very small part, if any, of what is really important to them. The reason is that most people are seldom consciously aware of the real motivations which drive their decision-making processes. And when they are, they are more inclined to protect that information than reveal it.

Since this is such a critical area, the next chapter, "Surveying the Subliminal," is devoted entirely to methods of discovering both realized and unrealized motivations and then applying them to the persuasion process.

At this point, however, you might ask, "What about the political process and companies trying to get us to use their products through advertising? There's no bidirectional communications. It's strictly one-way." That statement couldn't be farther from the truth.

Politicians and advertisers conduct extensive (and expensive) marketing surveys to glean sophisticated data on the various demographics of those who will be exposed to their messages. By the time the politician gives a speech or the advertiser launches a campaign, they know exactly and for maximum effectiveness what their market wants to hear and see.

The second part of the definition, getting the person to actually take the desired action, can be the easier or more difficult, depending upon the method of persuasion. As any politician or advertiser will confirm, getting someone to agree with their platform or product is one thing. Getting their vote or purchase is another.

A Two-Level Process

Before anyone can understand how persuasion influences decision-making, it is necessary first to understand how the human mind functions during that process.

In the simplest terms, it operates at two levels, the conscious and the subconscious, or subliminal. While the conscious mind concerns itself with our daily tasks and activities, the subconscious or subliminal mind functions below our level of awareness, continually focused upon physical survival and the various drives and motivations which have been programmed into us since birth.

The most basic example of this is breathing. We are not consciously aware of or concerned with breathing, nor do we have to concentrate on taking every breath and then exhaling it. If suddenly our supply of air is cut off, however, we become consciously aware of the situation and concerned with finding a new source.

The same is true of hunger. While it is possible to become so involved in something that we might temporarily forget about eating, it would be virtually impossible to forget about it to the point that we would starve to death. When our body needs more fuel, the subconscious or subliminal simply sends out a signal called hunger. If our body requires a certain substance, it sends a different signal, which we interpret as having "a taste" for something.

Subliminal Programming

In addition to our physical needs, the subconscious or subliminal mind also concentrates on what it considers our emotional needs and drives for survival.

Beginning with birth, and programmed in a manner very similar to that of a computer, its main concern is the physical survival of the infant. At this point in human development there are only four innate fears: of falling, loud noises, starvation, and isolation or deprivation. All are considered possible threats to survival and, as any new parent knows, are immediately and loudly signaled regardless of the time of day or night. This is why an infant generally has more curiosity than fear. It will play with anything that happens to be available, from a snake to a burning fire, because fears other than the basic four have yet to be programmed.

As the individual grows older, however, both positive and negative experiences and programming cause additional fears, anxieties, and prejudices, some of which are legitimate and necessary for survival but many of which become totally unfounded hindrances to the individual's progress.

Unfortunately, programming which takes place in the subconscious does not discriminate on the basis of logic, reality, or fact. Once in place, like a computer software program, the subconscious will continue to operate on that basis until new input replaces the old information.

$$2 + 2 = 5$$

For example, let's say that as part of a computer program the numbers two plus two are designated to equal five. Regardless of the validity of all other formulas or equations, computations will always be incorrect until the two-plus-two designation is corrected.

The same is true of the subconscious or subliminal human mind.

As an example, place a board twelve inches wide on the ground and walk the length of it. After doing this several times, you know logically that you are easily capable of accomplishing this without worrying about losing your balance or stepping off the board.

Now place the board a hundred feet in the air and do the same thing. On the basis of simple logic, you know you can walk the length of the board. You've already done it. But suddenly everything takes on a different perspective which has nothing whatsoever to do with logic. It's called fear.

Fear Is Nature's Way of Maintaining a Balance Between Bravery and Stupidity

Often expressed in the form of "what ifs," fear causes you to stop and think before doing something that might present a danger to survival. What if I lose my balance? What if a sudden gust of wind comes along? What if I slip? What if I lose my concentration?

Trainers of circus performers will tell you that the only way to eliminate this fear is to walk the length of the board over and over again, raising its height off the ground little by little. Reprogramming and the elimination of fear is eventually accomplished in the subliminal through repetition of positive and successful reinforcement.

Negative reinforcement is also programmed by repetition. If, for example, a child or adult is told on a continuing basis that he or she is worthless, ugly, and undeserving of anything, that notion becomes a main part of that individual's programming in the overall scheme of survival and is eventually accepted as fact. Until an effective modification is made in the individual's programming, assuming it is ever made, that person's actions, decisions, and direction in life will be based upon a program of low self-esteem and self-worth, even though it has no validity.

Most interesting about this is that while those actions and

decisions may appear to be made consciously, they are actually manifestations of the subconscious.

It is a well-known fact that people who as children were abused and/or molested by one or both parents have a tendency to abuse their spouses and children when they become adults. This is a result of negative programming during their childhood. Without any basis in fact, logic, or experience, their subliminal eventually accepted the abuse as perfectly normal behavior. When they become adults, the abuse is still part of their programming and quickly surfaces as a reality in their family life, causing a terrible conflict. After each episode they may invariably express sincere and heartfelt regret with promises that it will never happen again. When the behavior recurs, they will usually say something along the lines of, "I don't know what came over me. Something just snapped inside."

What "snapped" is their programming.

Although they know precisely what events precipitate their abusive response and are completely conscious of what they are doing, they will continue to be unable to control themselves until such time as professional help can effect reprogramming.

Another example of the power of the subliminal is illustrated in the case of a nurse who was grossly overweight. Although she made efforts to reduce through a number of programs, nothing, including prescription medication, seemed to have a lasting effect. She would lose weight at the initial stages, but after a short time gain back not only the weight she lost but additional pounds. As a nurse, she was especially aware of the danger she was courting. She desperately wanted to lose weight, yet was unable to control her eating frenzies.

Realizing she was on the verge of a mental and physical breakdown, her physician referred her to a psychologist who specialized in the treatment of addictions with the use of hypnosis and visualization therapy. Refusing to simply treat the external symptoms, as had been done by physicians in previous attempts, the psychologist used hypnotic regression therapy in an attempt to learn the basis of the problem.

Helping the young woman regress to a very early age, the psychologist discovered that as a child she suffered from a debilitating disease which placed her in and out of near-coma states. At that time, a doctor told her parents, "We can feed her intravenously for a while, but after that it will be up to you to get her eating and keep her eating to stay alive."

Her subconscious mind heard him and at that very moment a subliminal program was put in place, and her subconscious continued to direct her eating habits throughout the years, regardless of the fact that the danger of the disease had passed. In other words, two plus two equals five.

Once the psychologist accomplished the necessary deprogramming and subsequent reprogramming, the woman easily lost the weight and developed an entirely new attitude toward food.

As a result of research done in hundreds of cases with even more serious consequences, surgeons are now being trained to be extremely careful of verbalizations during surgery even though their patients are deeply anesthetized.

If you haven't already guessed, you might be asking yourself the question, "So what does all this have to do with persuasion?" The answer is: everything!

Motivators & Satisfiers

As we have seen, the primary concern of the subconscious or subliminal mind is the continuing survival of the individual. As the person grows older, however, other emotional objectives develop as a result of experiences.

For our purposes, we will call those objectives

Motivators

These are the driving emotional forces behind decisions and actions.

PRIME MOTIVATORS

survival/food/shelter

SECONDARY MOTIVATORS

ego	*greed*
vanity	*security*
love	*envy*
anger/hostility	*pride*
acceptance/approval by others	*attraction to pleasure*
aversion to pain/loss/rejection	*maternal instinct*

It is important to note that motivators vary in degree of importance from one person to another depending on the individual's experiences, personality, and programming.

To illustrate this, an individual who since childhood is constantly ridiculed, criticized, and beaten down may develop anger or hostility as a motivator, combined with pride, envy, and greed, the goal being to prove to the world that he or she is actually worthy of acceptance. Another individual in that same situation may go to the opposite extreme in a quest for acceptance by becoming docile and servile with no leanings whatsoever toward pride, anger, or hostility.

In both examples, while the initial programming was the same, the motivators and subsequent outward manifestations of motivators were different. Those manifestations we'll call

SATISFIERS.

Satisfiers can be any number of outward physical or emotional signs or clues subconsciously designated to meet the needs of motivators or a combination of motivators.

The drive for money, for example, is not a motivator because it is not a goal unto itself. It is simply the outward manifestation of a satisfier which identifies subliminal motivators or a combination of motivators at work within that person. Those might include ego, greed, vanity, attraction to pleasure, acceptance, or security.

To another individual, money may have absolutely no meaning whatsoever as a satisfier. This person might be addicted to the smell of smoking credit cards as they willingly rush headlong into hock, purchasing clothes, cars, jewelry, or whatever else trips their trigger, satisfying the very same motivators as the first person.

Interestingly enough, secondary motivators can and often do override even the prime motivator of survival. Take again the example of the board, this time putting it a hundred feet in the air with a teenager standing at one end and a group of his friends below. As they coax him to walk the length of the board, his subliminal mind has instilled tremendous fear (survival). But if he is heavily motivated by the need for acceptance and aversion to rejection, survival becomes subordinate and he may attempt the feat, knowing full well that he might die in the process.

In another example, the danger of breast implants has been extensively publicized and during one period the procedure was completely banned while the possibility of cancer and other medical side effects was investigated. Yet extensive numbers of women continued to undergo implants and even demanded "underground" procedures if necessary, strictly for cosmetic reasons. The prime motivator of survival in those instances became subordinate to ego, acceptance, vanity, and/or any number of combinations of secondary motivators.

The "gang syndrome" is yet another example. When interviewed by psychologists, psychiatrists, and social workers, gang members expressed shame and even rejection of crimes in which they participated, but felt compelled to carry them out in return for feelings of "belonging" and "family" not available to them in their homes.

While each of these examples illustrates the incredibly powerful role motivators and satisfiers play in the decision-making and persuasion process of the human psyche, there are relatively few professional people who realize or appreciate how effectively these driving forces can be employed.

Persuasion by Formula vs. Persuasion by Accident

Everyone has succeeded at one time or another in persuading someone to think or do something to which at first that person may have been totally opposed. Afterwards, they may have wondered how they accomplished such a feat. This is often the case with salespeople. Invariably, their ego leaps forward with the answer, usually directly related to one of the myths.

"You were able to turn that person around by making them feel important and then establishing yourself as a trusted friend. Your enthusiasm and excitement were contagious and they were caught up in it. Your positive mental attitude overpowered them. Your presentation was so smooth that they couldn't resist. You're simply one helluva closer. You created the need, then found the solution to their problem. You established yourself as the picture of success."

HOGWASH!

Actually, without being aware of it, they accidentally tripped across one or more of that person's motivators and/or satisfiers during the process of the presentation, rang the bell, and won the prize, which is what I did for years, then told myself how incredible I was—not with any measure of consistency, however, because I was operating on a format of accident, pointing a shotgun and then hoping like hell that I might hit something once in a while.

As an analogy, it's like following a recipe or formula. If you have all the ingredients and purposely or accidentally use them in the right order, you succeed. If you use them in the wrong order, however, you end up with a mess and might even hurt yourself in the process. If you shape ground meat into a patty with your hands and then broil or fry it, you end up with a hamburger. But just try frying the ground meat first and then forming it into a patty with your hands and see what happens.

It's the same with persuasion. If you have all the ingredients without the knowledge to apply them in the proper sequence, the formula is useless. On the other hand, if you have a formula for persuasion with all the necessary ingredients, and the knowledge and skill to implement those ingredients in the proper sequence, the result will always be consistent, with only a few exceptions due to the human factor or circumstances beyond your control.

The Formula for Persuasion

Realizing how powerful motivators are in influencing a person's decisions, the first step to persuasion is the process of learning which motivators and related satisfiers serve as the basis for a particular individual's decisions and actions.

The second step in the formula is communicating, in both the verbal and subliminal language your subject understands, exactly how your product, service, idea, or opinion not only relates to but also fulfills the requirements of their primary motivators and satisfiers.

The third step, realizing that agreement represents only part of the definition of the persuasion process, is to initiate the response or action you desire.

And the fourth step is reassuring the decision to firmly implant and reinforce the reprogramming you have accomplished, similar to raising the board a few feet at a time as the individual walks its length.

While these four steps may sound logical and relatively easy to accomplish, they involve more intricacy than might be imagined. In the first step, for example, if different satisfiers can indicate the same motivators, and vice versa, how do you tell the difference? The simple solution is to ask!

Unfortunately, the majority of people do not know the driving motivators behind their decision-making process and, if they do, generally refuse to admit to it. How many people, for example, are likely to divulge that they are driven by greed, envy, vanity, aversion to rejection or the need for acceptance? And if confronted with those motivations, in those very words, how likely do you think it is that you would be able to persuade them of anything before they cause you bodily injury?

The only way to discover the truth is by knowing first what to ask, and second *how to ask it,* otherwise known as . . .

SURVEYING THE SUBLIMINAL

4

SURVEYING THE SUBLIMINAL

The gurus typically preach the necessity of a planned, "canned" presentation based upon the theory that through repetition it eventually becomes detailed, smooth, and natural.

This is about as effective as a football team practicing only one offensive play formation. It may work once or twice, but what happens throughout the rest of the game? What happens when you're playing against a team with an entirely different strategy?

The "Planning Ahead" Trap

The first critical mistake people make in the persuasion process is planning in advance exactly how and what they're going to say to their subject. They'll stand in front of mirrors, use tape recorders, and practice their presentation much like an actor rehearsing a play.

The process of persuasion, however, is not a theatrical production and all the players don't follow the same script. If you're working on a special project and decide you need additional people, you might plan in detail exactly how you're going to request your supervisor's approval to hire them. Once your entire speech is prepared, memorized, and rehearsed, you walk into the office and the first words out of your supervisor's mouth are, "I hope that project is almost finished. We're working on a very tight budget as it is, you know."

A match has just been set to your carefully prepared script and the blood drains from your face as you stammer and stutter to come up with another excuse for being there.

Or assume you're selling computer systems and a customer walks in the door telling you his old equipment is outmoded and he's looking for a replacement. This is the moment you've been anticipating. All the hours of practice and study are finally going to pay off and you can picture the commission going into your checking account as you sweep him across the floor to the magnificent new Megabucks 8000. Within seconds, your fingers become a blur on the keyboard as you show him all the incredible features of the machine, how it will perform fifteen functions simultaneously, and all the complicated programs it will run, not to mention how intelligent and well versed you are in computer terminology and language.

Finally, you conclude your demonstration. "And just think, you get all this for only nine thousand, nine hundred ninety-five dollars because it happens to be on sale this week. Isn't that a great deal!"

Suddenly you glance at him and notice his blank stare at the monitor and the vacant expression on his face. At that instant, the idea that something just might be wrong wiggles its way past the thoughts of how you're going to spend the commission.

"Uh, well, I was looking for something simpler and a lot less expensive," he says, embarrassed. "Maybe around three thousand."

"Three . . . three thousand, did you say? Oh sure," you agree, seeing dollars sliding out of your account. "I just wanted to show you some of the latest technology, that's all."

At this point you feel like the sleeping cat that's just fallen off a nice, warm TV set and nonchalantly starts cleaning itself as if that was really the plan from the beginning.

"Why not step over here and take a look at our Chintz 286, which I'm sure will handle what you need," you say, a small tremor of dread in your voice because you just about know what's coming next.

"Well, this is really nice," he says after seeing the demo, "but it doesn't do all the neat things like the other one you showed me. Actually, they're both a little too complicated for me anyway. I'll tell you what . . . maybe I'll just look around and give you a call after I get a chance to read up on all this new stuff." He walks out the door along with any hopes you might have had for a sale. The truth is, you'll never see the guy again, much less get a telephone call from him.

If you believe this is an exaggerated example, think about the last time you talked yourself into a corner only to discover you weren't even in the right room. It happens all the time.

As discussed in the last chapter, to effectively present any idea, opinion, product, or service for the greatest possible acceptance, the first objective is to discover the satisfiers and motivators of those to whom it is directed, keeping in mind that they vary in both degree and combination from one individual to another.

So how do we find out what satisfiers and motivators trip a specific person's decision-making, action-initiating triggers?

Ask and You Shall Receive

That's simple. The trick is how.

The survey is one of the most crucial yet commonly neglected of all phases of persuasion, especially in the selling profession. In fact, only one in ten salespeople (there's that familiar 10 percent figure again) knows how to conduct it effectively or, for that matter, does it at all.

A common complaint among real estate agents is spending days with a prospective buyer, "becoming close friends," only to discover that they purchased a home within hours of meeting another agent.

Unbelievable? Not really. Walk into a real estate office and announce that you're looking for a home.

"And what size home would that be?" asks the agent on floor duty.

You say that you're looking for a two-bedroom, two-bath home with a two-car garage. The next question will be the price range. And that's usually the end of the survey.

The typical agent (90 percent of them) will immediately jump to the MLS listings, pick four or five homes for starters, and whisk you off on a tour of several neighborhoods. While driving, the agent will engage you in pleasant conversation to learn what you do, how many kids you have, etc., etc. As you walk through each home the agent will attempt to learn, through the process of elimination, what you like and dislike, while wasting time, gas, and your patience, hoping to eventually stumble upon the house of your dreams.

After several days of this, conversation dwindles and irritability rises as you realize your agent still hasn't a clue to what you really want. Once your patience has run its course, you go to another who, if you're lucky, sits you down, asks some very pertinent questions, and takes you to two, three, or maybe even four homes which fit your specifications. At that point, the decision is yours.

Upon learning of your purchase, the first agent—your "buddy"—will be absolutely devastated.

"I can't imagine how you could do that to me after I spent so much time with you! I really began to feel we were so close!" (See myth #6.)

Yet, if you were to suggest that he or she use the method of selection employed by the agent from whom you purchased the home, the response would be, "Oh no, you really don't understand. This is real estate. You just don't do that in this business."

Exactly. That's what it is. A business. And people aren't in a real estate office, or for that matter any office, to make new friends. If that's what they wanted, they'd join a social club.

People go to offices because they want something, and whether they know precisely what it is or not, it is the persuader's job to discover it.

The Subliminal Survey:
Avenue to Discovery

Regardless of whether you're selling a product, idea, or, in the case of a job interview, yourself, the most important part of that sale is the survey.

People, when given the opportunity, will always tell you their desires and how they expect to attain them as long as you treat them as individuals, ask the right questions in the proper manner, and listen closely to their answers. The difficult part is to know *what* questions to ask, *why* you're asking them, and more importantly, *how* they should be asked to get a definitive answer without alienating the subject by appearing to conduct an interrogation.

Since people are usually more comfortable answering questions from an interview sheet than on a face-to-face basis, the most important tool is a piece of paper, preferably one that already has your questions on it, and a pen to take notes. This "form approach" depersonalizes the nature of questions even when asked by a total stranger. In order to be effective, however, it must be introduced properly.

"Mr. Jones, before we get into a discussion of (my product, my idea, me) would you mind if I ask a few questions just to make sure I have an accurate idea of what's important to you?"

Are you asking a question here? Yes, but more significantly, you're conveying a number of statements to this person which will later make your ability to persuade more effective.

Described in more detail in the chapter "Verbal Subliminal Persuasion," what you're really saying is, "I'm putting *your*

needs and interests before my own. I am an extremely detailed
and thorough individual and I feel *your opinions* are *important*.
I *respect* you and therefore am requesting *your permission* to ask
some questions, the answers to which are *important* enough
that I'm willing to write them down."

Important, Important, Important

Do you know anyone who does not appreciate feeling important?

As you ask your questions and take notes on the answers,
you compound that person's importance and will quickly find
them going into more and more detailed responses. The more
detail they give you, the easier it will be to discover the various
motivators and satisfiers to which your presentation should be
directed to maximize effective persuasion. It is also critical at
this point to realize that what people say and what they really
mean can be 180 degrees apart, the accurate interpretation of
which is also detailed in the next chapter.

For now, however, there are basic rules to keep in mind when
conducting the survey.

Rule #1: Most of Us Were Born with Twice the Number of Eyes and Ears as Mouths for a Reason.

As a country involved in international relations, a business in
marketing strategies, or individuals in personal relationships,

we would all be better off paying more attention to this advice. In short, if we spent twice as much time listening to other people as we did talking, we would have a much better idea what to say and how to really communicate with them when we do open our mouths.

The Difference Between Listening and Hearing

People are generally more interested in hearing their own voice expressing their own opinions than listening to others. Afterwards, they wonder how their audience could possibly be so stupid as to misunderstand their perfectly rational point of view expressed in such eloquent terms.

Did you ever notice while speaking to someone that they seem to be fidgeting, looking away, nodding, and mumbling, "Uh-huh, uh-huh." Consciously, subconsciously, or both, you become aware that while they appear to be hearing and agreeing with you, they're not listening. In fact, by nodding and mumbling agreement, they're making it obvious that they'd prefer it if you'd just shut up so they can say something really important. While you're talking, they're planning what they want to say the moment you stop, can hardly wait for the opportunity to express their own point of view, and will even interrupt you if you continue too long. They are hearing your voice, but not *listening*.

Based upon that, what importance are you going to place on what they have to say? Neither knowing nor caring about your point of view, is there any chance they will be able to persuade you of anything?

Only by *listening* to another person, *interpreting* what they are really expressing, *learning* their point of view and the specific way they communicate is it then possible to present our own ideas in such a manner that others will not only understand but *agree* and then act in the manner we desire. That's called persuasion.

Rule #2: The Most Important Word in Anyone's Vocabulary Is Their Own Name.

What happens when you hear your name? You naturally respond by paying attention. Your name is special, singling you out from everyone else.

That's why using a person's name is so critical during the survey as well as the persuasion process. Not only do you keep their attention, but it encourages them to respond to you.

When people introduce themselves to you, they are giving you a "handle" by which to refer to them. How they do it signals, in part, the formality they expect. In our so-called casual society, the use of first names is common. Do not make the mistake, however, of believing this is acceptable to everyone.

Someone introducing her- or himself with only a first name is obviously giving you permission to use it. This is not necessarily the case when the introduction includes both first and last names. In this instance, a good rule to follow is to use the last name preceded by Mr. or Ms. until such time as the person tells you to use the first name or it's comfortable to ask if they'd mind you using their first name. If there is any hesitation at all, quickly bypass the question and continue with the last name.

If, however, a person introduces him- or herself as Mr. Smith or Ms. Jones, they are obviously displaying their choice to keep things on a purely business basis. Under no circumstance should permission to use the first name even be requested. If during the course of the conversation they wish to change the relationship, they will initiate it.

Rule #3: Everyone Listens to Station WIIFM—All the Time!

People like to think the days of the "me first generation" are gone. In reality, that attitude has never diminished but instead become more predominant than ever.

When presented with anything, the foremost thought in the mind of the subject is, "What's in it for me? Will I feel, look, or be better off because of it? What can I hope to get out of it for myself?"

Producers of political and product commercials pay for expensive marketing demographics to determine what the largest percentage of the American public wants to hear for their individual benefit. They want to be popular, beautiful, have fun, and be carefree. Drink this beer and you can have it all. Men and women want to lose weight, be fit, trim, and attractive to the opposite sex.

"You know you can't do it yourself and if you could it would take work, time, and self-control, so join this program and you'll dump the fat for only a dollar a pound, quickly, easily, and with no effort on your part."

People want to hear about low-cost medical, child care, and employment programs, while at the same time having more leisure time and spendable income because their taxes will be cut. So vote for this person regardless of their previous political record.

Does anyone really believe the people in the commercials maintain their muscle-toned bodies by swilling beer all day? Does anyone really believe you drop weight and then maintain weight loss forever without exercise or proper eating habits? Does anyone really trust any promises given by a politician running for office?

The answer is NO! But do they buy the products and cast their vote because of the benefits they really want to believe will apply to them personally? The answer is YES.

Because everyone listens to WIIFM.

Once you learn what someone wants to hear and then how to apply what you are presenting from the perspective of what's in it for them, you are well on the way to accomplishing persuasion.

"Typing" on the Subliminal Keyboard

If you've ever used a computer, you've learned that it operates on the basis of a program in which a specific command always triggers the same result regardless of the number of times or circumstances under which you give it. If you don't know the exact command, you simply backtrack. Look at the result, find the command that issued that specific result, open the directory of other commands, and you'll find the original operating system or program.

People are no different.

As already seen in the previous chapter, we, like computers, also operate on the basis of subliminal motivator programming which issues commands called satisfiers. Once issued, those commands yield the same results over and over again.

To find the program, you simply backtrack. Look at the result, find the satisfier that caused the result, look at the directory of other satisfiers, and you'll discover the motivator. Simply put, to discover how a person will be persuaded to do something in the future, find out how they were persuaded to do something similar in the past. Similar to psychological testing batteries, the survey is designed to help you pinpoint the various motivators and satisfiers precipitating a decision and subsequent action, which is why it is so effective.

In a real estate example, the properly conducted survey addresses itself to people as individuals, pinpointing reasons he, she, or the two of them together will purchase a particular home. This is done without spinning wheels, wasting gas, and going through an irritating, slow, ineffective, and completely inaccurate process of elimination.

The first step is to invite the subjects into a private office. This is a business, and being potential clients, they are special.

Second, request permission to ask "a few questions just to make sure I have an accurate idea of what's important to you."

Third, *how* you ask the questions is as important as the questions themselves. In conjunction with the "form survey" you should ask them lightly and conversationally without sounding like an interrogator but also conveying that the answers are important enough that you take notes.

The key questions in this example are:

"Would you mind telling me where you live now? That's a very nice area. Just out of curiosity, what was it that impressed you about the area when you first moved there? What kind of home do you have? How long have you lived there? If you were to single out the most important reasons you originally purchased your home, what would they be? Is there anything about your present home that you don't like? Why is it that you're thinking of moving now? Obviously, if you're thinking of moving to a new home, you have some idea what you'd like. What would that be? What would you say are the most important factors related to making a decision on the type of home you'd purchase? How much of a factor will price play in that decision?"

These are just a few of the questions which stimulate responses during a survey conversation, none of which allow a simple yes or no answer. As a result, you'll learn more than just the type of home they might purchase.

About what are they most defensive and most open? What are their turnoffs and turn-ons? What is it about a home that they really consider important? Do they agree on those factors, or is there disagreement between them? What kind of life do they lead as opposed to the kind of life they want to lead? What do they want to portray to others?

What are their *real motivators*?

Although this example illustrates a real estate survey, the same format of questioning applies to an interview with a prospective employer, a supervisor to whom you want to present an idea, or someone to whom you might want to be closer on a personal basis. Common sense dictates that in the case of the latter, suddenly pulling out a prepared survey sheet would hardly be appropriate. Not only would it be counterproductive to informality, it might also lead to serious questions about your motives, if not your sanity. The actual questioning process, however, is similarly effective.

If, for example, you know the person was in a previous relationship, you could ask in the proper context of conversation what he or she found appealing about that person when they first met. What type of things did they like to do together? What makes him or her really feel close to or romantic with someone? If he or she met the ideal person, what would make that person so perfect?

Answers to questions like these, questions which pertain directly to emotions felt and subsequent decisions made in the past, point to a pattern of programming for future emotions and decisions.

The most important thing to keep in mind is that the only way to effectively persuade anyone to do or feel anything is to know under what circumstances and information *they want to do it.*

The completed survey shows you how to focus your presentation to meet that end. It gives you the direction, strategy, and course to follow in presenting your product, idea, or yourself during the next step:

VERBAL SUBLIMINAL PERSUASION

5

VERBAL SUBLIMINAL PERSUASION

Once the formal survey has been completed, you should have the basis upon which to carefully and strategically direct your approach in presenting your idea to the subject. It is important, however, that you do so with flexibility to allow for any contradiction of information gained during the survey which might have been misinterpreted on your part or, as is frequently the case, purposely misrepresented or hidden by the subject.

The primary objective at this stage is to introduce your idea, opinion, product, or service as attractively and desirably as possible in conforming with the subject's motivational and satisfier profile.

This is accomplished with a wide variety of techniques detailed throughout the remainder of this book, beginning with verbal communication, not only as it pertains to the persuader but also to how you interpret comments and responses from the subject.

"You Should Have Known That Wasn't What I Meant!"

Spoken words are among the most indistinct, vague, and mis-interpreted communication in all relationships, both business and personal, and represent one of the major stumbling blocks to effective persuasion.

As we have already seen, people often don't listen to each other and, when they do, don't really hear what the other person is actually saying—almost the equivalent of two people talking to each other in different foreign languages, which, as you'll see, is generally the case even though they're both speaking English.

The reason is that what someone says, what they mean, what you hear, and what you think they mean can have four entirely different interpretations. That's why reliance solely on verbal communication is confusing, misleading, and most often disastrous.

Politicians are unchallenged in this arena. Who else, for example, can answer a question without really addressing it and leave you wondering whether they actually responded to it? If they ever spoke in plain English there would be no need for so-called commentators "analyzing" a political speech immediately after it airs on television.

"The president said this or that, implying such and such, but what do you think he really meant, Susan?" asks one of the anchors.

"Well, John, why don't we take that to our panel of experts and see what they have to say," she responds as the picture flips to a group of three people who appear to be very dignified and professional with notebooks and pens. After formal introductions, titles, and credits, they immediately dissect the speech, explaining in depth meanings associated with sentences, phrases, and even specific words.

Why, you wonder, does it frequently take more time to "analyze" what the president said than it took to present the entire speech, especially since you've just heard it? Do they think you're deaf, stupid, or a combination of both? To learn the answer to that, change the channel and receive a totally different analysis.

It's the job of commentators to both interpret and slant the meaning of a politician's statements to match their particular station's political profile. Depending on what they want to persuade the viewing public to believe, one station's commentators will give you an entirely different analysis than another's. And since politicians rarely address any question with a specifically direct answer, any station's analysis can have a valid basis.

That's why among all forms of communication, experts agree that only 8 percent is based upon actual words, 32 percent on voice inflection, and 60 percent on body language.

Say the Secret Words to Win!

In sales, a "green pea" will often ask a veteran producer, "Would you tell me what you say to get people to agree with you?

When do you give prices, at the beginning or end? How do you present the benefits, and which ones do you emphasize?"

Generally the veteran will answer that it's always different depending on the circumstances or prospect. Soon after, the rumor will circulate that the top producer obviously has a secret presentation he or she wouldn't divulge under pain of death.

The reason I know is because I've been on both sides of that fence. As a novice, I was always trying to discover that secret presentation until one of the top producers actually invited me to go with him on an appointment. Just to make sure I'd get it down pat, I even concealed a small, high-sensitivity tape recorder. Unfortunately, because I didn't know how to really analyze the tape afterwards, it turned out to be even more confusing because I thought he said almost exactly the same things I did in my presentation, but with very different results.

I couldn't have been more mistaken.

If I had really listened, I would have noticed that while he used almost the same words in generally the same order that I did, his emphasis, intonation, and inflection were totally different from mine. If I had *listened* and heard what he said, I would have learned something to put me on the right path years before it actually happened.

If you doubt this for even a moment, consider the statement

"I didn't say he misrepresented his product."

Seeing this in writing, it seems straightforward enough. Verbally, however, that's hardly the case. As an experiment, read the sentence aloud, putting emphasis on the italicized word.

"*I* didn't say he misrepresented his product."

This implies, "I didn't say it but someone else did."

"I *didn't* say he misrepresented his product."

The interpretation here is, "Why are you accusing me of saying something I never said? The fact is I didn't say it and that's final!"

"I didn't *say* he misrepresented his product."

"I didn't say it, I wrote it in a letter," or "I didn't actually say it, but I did imply that was the case."

"I didn't say *he* misrepresented his product."

"I didn't say he did it but someone else sure did. In any case, whoever did it, the product was misrepresented."

"I didn't say he *misrepresented* his product."

"He didn't exactly misrepresent the product, but I'm certainly not happy with it," or "Although I couldn't actually prove misrepresentation it sure doesn't perform the way I thought it would."

"I didn't say he misrepresented *his* product."

"It wasn't his product he misrepresented. It was someone else's he did a number on," or, worse yet, "It wasn't his that he misrepresented, it was yours!"

"I didn't say he misrepresented his *product*."

"It wasn't his product, it was the way it was supposed to perform," or "It wasn't the product that was misrepresented, it was him that I didn't like."

Considering that in one seven-word sentence there are a *minimum* of ten different interpretations, is there any question why verbal communication can be confusing at best?

Emphasis and voice inflection in the simplest statement play an important role in determining the mood, attitude, and subject's response pattern, which will continue throughout the rest of the discussion. In a question, intonation and emphasis are even more important and may well determine whether rapport is established or instantly destroyed, either enforcing or negating the entire persuasion process. Based not upon not the question itself, but *how it is asked* and then perceived by the subject, a simple question asked out of curiosity might be interpreted as an insult or accusation.

For example, assume that part of your survey requires some information regarding the subject's income. Asking this simple question could have a number of implications, all of which depend upon intonation and emphasis.

"*What* was your income last year?"

"What *was* your income last year?"

"What was *your* income last year?"

"What was your *income* last year?"

"What was your income *last* year?"

"What was your income last *year?*"

Reading aloud each of the questions with emphasis on the italicized word, as you did in the first example, it becomes easy to understand that it's not the question itself but rather the *im-*

plication as interpreted by the subject which will set different moods and responses.

Based upon your delivery, he or she may answer the question willingly, grudgingly, with an outright lie, or in the worst case, ask you who you think you are and tell you it's none of your damn business!

If the latter is true, you'd probably be correct in assuming that rapport has been somewhat impaired, to put it mildly. Rewording this question not only neutralizes it but also provides a solid foundation for rapport when done properly.

"There's a space I have to fill out on this survey regarding income, primarily for the benefit of our marketing department. Now, I realize that it's really none of my business, the company's, or anyone else's for that matter, but if you wouldn't mind, would you please give me a number to fill in here? Whatever comes to mind would be fine."

What does it *sound like* you're really saying?

First, that you're simply doing your job filling out a company form; that being an employee of the company, the question isn't your idea; that you're courteous enough to realize the delicate area you're in; that you'd really appreciate it if your prospect would help you do your job; and that you personally don't really care if he tells you the truth. In fact, you *don't* care, because in reality you're on his side!

Wording the question in this manner, as an almost trivial request which requires no defensive action on the subject's part, actually gives you a better chance of getting the truth.

If the person is the type who would lie about their income, they would do so regardless of how the question was asked or the answer demanded. By downplaying it, however, you at least don't run the risk of destroying rapport.

Ya Gotta Say It with En-Thu-Siasm!

Enthusiasm (myth #4) in intonation, inflection, and emphasis is also critical to persuasion.

If you've ever attended "motivational" seminars, you've undoubtedly noticed that when the gurus talk about enthusiasm, it's always in a very loud tone of voice. In fact, the word itself is always spoken with a louder than normal emphasis on the second syllable.

En-*thu*-siasm!

For some unexplained reason, this is supposed to create excitement. In fact, one of the oldest myths in the selling field is the statement "There is nothing as catching or that sells more than enthusiasm!"

That makes about as much sense as raising your voice when speaking to a blind person. Is it reasonable? Not at all, but a person who is blind will tell you it's common.

People Like People Who Are Like Themselves

Human beings relate to people who are similar to them in personality, values, outlook on life, and attitudes toward acceptable behavior—in other words, people who are like themselves.

To see the truth of this in action, do another experiment. (Be forewarned, however, and do not do it with anyone with whom you think you might like a relationship, in a job interview, or in a selling situation.) Find a person who generally tends to be conservative in nature. An engineer, chemist, accountant, or computer programmer/analyst will usually fit this profile perfectly. Go right up to within a foot or two of him with a big smile on your face and your hand stuck out, grab his hand in a firm grip, hammer it up and down like you're priming a pump, and proclaim in a loud, en-thu-siastic voice, "Hey, Mr. Jones, my name is John Doe! I've really been looking forward to meeting you! Have you got a couple minutes to sit down and talk together? Boy, I'd sure appreciate it!"

How do you think he'd respond? How do you think he'd feel? Do you think for a minute he'd be comfortable or at ease with you? Or could you more easily picture the blood draining from his face and his eyes widening with fear as he steps back, attempting to jerk his hand from your grip?

Save yourself the embarrassment of this experiment. There would be absolutely no need to go further because any possibility of rapport, communication, and subsequent persuasion would have been shattered. You'd have proven beyond any doubt that your personality is not only quite different from his but also one he would neither like nor appreciate.

The reason is because Mr. Jones's idea of enthusiasm is quite different from what he would see as the loudmouthed, pushy, and phony person you'd portray.

Another illustration might well be found in your own family. If you know anyone who is a slow, methodical morning riser and likes to shuffle to the kitchen, set up the coffee, and not even listen to the news until the first cup is poured, just see how they might react to someone who leaps out of bed, throws open the curtains, and cheerily proclaims what an absolutely Great Day it is!

Homicide has been committed for less, and divorce is common!

Interestingly enough, the personality traits shown above, which some people like to refer to as "outgoing," might be just the right ticket for someone who acts and thinks similarly. Until you know for sure, however, you might be digging yourself a hole you can never climb out of, turning the person off to you and whatever you might have to say throughout the balance of your discussion. Beginning an introduction conservatively always gives you the latitude to be more outgoing.

It's the wise persuaders who not only listen but hear, not only see but watch the people they're talking to before opening their mouths.

The Hidden Meanings of Words

Specific words can also have a subliminally beneficial or detrimental effect. If, for example, you happen to be attempting to persuade someone to make a timely decision, consider the inevitable result of the following statements.

"Ms. Smith, I'd like you to *think about* the many ways this plan will work for you."

"I'd really appreciate it if you would *think about* giving me the new position."

"What do you *think about* this fantastic price we are offering?"

"Just *think about* the variety of applications this would have for your business."

"What do you *think about* my ideas for expansion?"

Is there any reason in the world, after subliminally pounding those words into Ms. Smith's head, that you should be surprised when she finally says, "This is really great and I see where it has advantages, but first I want to *think about* it before making a decision."

This is the point at which people bemoan the inability of others to make a decision. They might call Ms. Smith ignorant, stupid, inattentive, or indecisive, question her legitimate ancestry, or affix animal descriptions to her personality, never realizing that she did exactly what they told her to do—think about it!

On the other side of the coin, there are subliminally positive words and phrases which, when properly used, also prompt the listener to do exactly as told.

"*Today* it's important that we . . ."

"You can surely understand why *today* it's really important to . . ."

"I'll show you *today* the various aspects of my idea which will . . ."

Repetitious use of the word *today* has a subliminal effect on the thought pattern of the person to whom it's directed, most especially in the final decision-making phase of the discussion or presentation.

Another subliminally effective and probably one of the most subtle methods of persuasion is using words which sound like you're saying one thing yet have an entirely different effect on the subconscious.

By now you might have an idea.

By now it's almost obvious.

By now you should realize what I'm actually saying.

BUY NOW it's obvious how this applies to persuasion in a selling situation!

The subject consciously understands the words "by now" to mean "at this point in our discussion." The subliminal, however, processes words in another meaning— "BUY NOW! BUY NOW! BUY NOW!"—especially if there is a conscious interest and if the product, service, or idea lends itself to the subject's motivational and satisfier profile.

I (See) (Hear) (Feel)
That What You're Saying Is . . .

As you undoubtedly understand at this point, specific words can have entirely different meanings and interpretations depending upon intonation and emphasis. They can also have different meanings depending on the people who hear them and how they process information upon which they will ultimately make decisions.

This is another reason verbal communication is often confusing at best, especially for those who are not aware of the distinctions.

Three different ways people process information are: visually, aurally, and kinesthetically. While everyone tends to use combinations of all three, one of these will always predominate, depending on the individual.

You might ask why this is being covered in "Verbal Subliminal Persuasion." Aural fits, but what about visual and kinesthetic? The reason is that the actual words people use most frequently reveal their primary information processing patterns.

The Visual Processor

The majority of people process information visually. They make decisions based upon what they see and most often express themselves with some of the following word clues:

see	*look(s)*	*point of view*	*discover*	*focus*
show	*appear*	*reveal*	*envision*	*expand*
clear	*crystal clear*	*hazy*	*flash*	*picture*
		illuminate		

Example: "From your *point of view*, does this *look* like something you could *see* yourself doing or is it still a little bit *hazy?*"

The Aural Processor

Aurally oriented people express themselves with different word clues:

hear	*listen*	*sounds like*	*in tune*	*all ears*
silence	*deaf*	*attuned to*	*harmony*	*tone*
crystal clear	*rings a bell*	*clear*		

Example: "Just to make sure this is *crystal clear* for you, does it *sound* like it's *in tune* with something you'd like to *hear* more about?"

(Notice the words *crystal clear* are used both visually and aurally. One pertains to seeing something, the other to hearing. Before jumping to one conclusion or the other, listen to other words a person most often uses.)

The Kinesthetic Processor

People who tend to process information kinesthetically reveal their processing pattern with predominant use of words such as:

feel	*touch*	*grab*	*handle*	*tap*
hold	*concrete*	*hard*	*contact*	*grasp*
slip	*slide*	*solid*	*fall into*	*miss*

Example: "Just so I know you've got a *handle* on this, do you *feel* the program is something which would be of *concrete* value as a *solid* investment for you?"

People generally understand your meaning regardless of whether you do or do not use terms they habitually prefer. When you use terminology explicit to their processing patterns, however, you have a distinct advantage in both communication and persuasion. You are more positively received speaking to them in their "language" as well as being more like them.

Remembering again that people like people who are like themselves: You can *show* a visual person what *appears* to be good for him or her if they can *see* your *point*. You are much more in *harmony* with an aural type when you *sound* like you're *attuned* to their wants. And a kinesthetic will have a better *grasp* of what you mean if you *hand* them *concrete* facts upon which to make a decision.

"Looking Out for Number One"

In Robert Ringer's book of the same title, he correctly states that if you don't look out for yourself, no one is going to do it for you. Few ever consider, however, that people they are trying to persuade are also looking out for number one!

In a futile attempt to "gain rapport during the warm-up" they talk about themselves, their experiences, life situations, beliefs, and opinions, hoping that somewhere in this haystack they will find a needle of commonality. Not yet having any knowledge of the subject at this early point, however, they are more likely to stumble across an area of dissimilarity, actually creating an initial barrier which will continue to be reinforced throughout the discussion.

Putting aside your ego can be a painful experience, but you must accept the fact that at the beginning of any discussion, the person sitting across the desk does not know you; does not want to know you; does not care about you, your opinion, your family, your circumstances, your kids' grades, your dog, your accomplishments, your problems, what you think, or what you say!

They only care about: their situation, their opinions, their

well-being, what they think and say, **and that you don't treat
them as if they are stupid enough to be unaware of what
you are trying to accomplish with phony small talk!**

Out of courtesy they may sit there listening attentively, smiling acquiescently, and nodding their head in agreement while
wondering if what you eventually say will provide a personal
benefit in the satisfaction of their motivators and satisfiers as
they listen to WIIFM.

Answering a Question
with a Question

One of the oldest lessons in the Guru Book of Selling is to always answer a question with a question. If the prospect asked,
"Does it come in green?" your instant response is supposed to
be "Do you want it in green?", thus "boxing" the person and
closing the sale.

That was then. This is now.

Today's sophisticated people have seen this technique used
over and over in everything from television law dramas to dealing with their children. When asking a question, they are in
essence again saying "What's in it for me?" and they want an
answer. Answering with a question simply leaves them with one
or both of two impressions: that you're trying to avoid the question because you can't come up with an answer; or that you're
trying to be cute, thereby insulting their intelligence.

Either impression breaks rapport. Together, they shatter it
completely.

Remember When . . .

Another technique the old school loves to use is called restatement. "Remember when I said before that . . ." Using this simply doesn't work because your subject didn't care about it when you said it, so why should anything be different now?

Restatement does work, however, when you put it another way. Referring openly to the survey, you ask, "Remember what you said to the questions I asked a little while ago? You said you wanted . . . Now let me show you how this applies exactly to what you said you want."

Now they care! Now they're paying attention! Since it applies to what they said, it therefore applies to what they want!

If you go one step further and restate it in the same manner and using the words they most frequently use to process information, you are now speaking their language and persuasion is well on the way.

Let Me See If I've Got This Right

At the end of the presentation, the subject will often make the statement, "OK, let me see if I've got this right," or "Let's just see if I really understand what you're suggesting to me," followed by a reiteration of the high points of the discussion.

THIS INDICATES A DECISION HAS ALMOST BEEN MADE—BUT IS ALSO A WARNING FLAG! What is really being said is one of two things.

The first is, "I'm sold on the idea provided everything is exactly the way you tell me and the results will be what I expect."

In this case, the subject has already decided to agree, but is scrutinizing the various aspects of what has been presented, looking for any contradictions. If none occur, persuasion has been accomplished successfully.

The second interpretation is, "I'm not really sure, but I think I see a flaw and I want to give you a chance to either confirm it or explain it away." Like most people, the subject wants reinforcement and final justification of a positive or negative decision which has almost but not yet been finalized.

Either interpretation requires the persuader to carefully listen from the point of view of the subject to exactly what this person is saying or asking, not merely in words but in their own language. And although intonation, inflection, and the use of different words represent a critical 40 percent of that language, the best, most fascinating, and effective part is yet to be explored:

NONVERBAL SUBLIMINAL PERSUASION

NONVERBAL SUBLIMINAL PERSUASION

I found out very early in life that my mother had magical powers.

After describing them to my little friends, an even bigger surprise was discovering that their mothers had those powers too, leading us all to the eventual conclusion that mothers were really good witches in disguise, a discovery which carried with it important responsibilities.

For one thing, you had to be careful what you thought about, because mothers could read your mind.

Like the day in third grade when, thinking like a lot of little boys do, I decided that since I was bored, everyone else must be too. Somebody just had to do something and since I was never one to shirk responsibility, I decided that the somebody had to be me. Looking around the room of twenty-some classmates, I reached into my pocket and pulled out the rubber band with which, through hours of practice, I had become deadly accurate firing precisely folded paper wads. In fact, there was only one other whose level of skill, speed, and accuracy even came close to mine. His name was Roger Gorski, and he was a swaggering, smirking, and particularly nasty-tempered individual, even for a third grader, who just happened to be two rows left and three desks ahead of me. He was the one nobody liked, taking particular enjoyment doing things for which the entire class would be punished when he alone was responsible, and I decided it was time he paid his dues.

That day, as luck would have it, he was looking out the window and suddenly the back of his head sent a shiver of excitement through me, probably much the same feeling a hunter gets when a deer is framed in the cross hairs of his rifle scope. Sister Mary Therese turned to write something on the board. A split second later, my missile was launched with blurring speed as it homed in on the target.

Bap! It smacked him dead center in the back of his head and he spun in his chair, the usual smirk now replaced by an angry grimace and flames of retaliation burning in his eyes. But by this time the rubber band was hidden in my clutched fist as I attentively watched the nun, just now turning to face the class.

"Roger!" she snapped. "The only thing you need to look at is going on right up here in front of the room. Now pay attention!"

Naturally, the next time the nun turned to the board, Roger loaded his rubber band and retaliated point-blank against a perfectly innocent bystander two desks behind him. Minutes later, when she turned to the board once more, a flurry of wads filled the air and the twang of rubber bands resounded in the room.

That got Sister's attention and she spun to confront the class. Standing up there with her fists clenched at her sides, her heels together, and an expression which left little doubt as to what was bound to happen next, I remember thinking that she resembled what I imagined an insanely angry penguin would look like, and I couldn't help the grin which twisted my face.

"He started it, Sister!"

Those words, shrieked in the high-pitched squeal I'd hated from the first day I heard it, struck my very soul. I turned to see Jennifer Putney, acknowledged teacher's pet and my personal nemesis, a satisfied grin on her face and her finger pointed directly at me.

The next thing I knew, I was lifted from the desk by my ear, that natural handle God provided nuns to steer little boys out of the room and down to the pastor's office for swift and terrible retribution I didn't even want to imagine.

When I arrived home after school that day, I was immediately heartened by the sound of my mother humming along with the radio, which put to rest the fear that the priest might have called her.

"Hi, honey, how was school today?" she asked, kissing my cheek.

This was the critical moment. Trying my level best to avoid thinking about what had happened at school and thus circumvent her magic mind-reading ability, I put on the most angelic smile I could muster. "Oh, just great!" I said, and for that little extra touch of drama, "We really learned a lot today!"

The pleasant expression slowly dissolved from her face.

"What happened?" she asked, and suddenly the tone of the question edged on accusation.

I was in trouble! *Total innocence,* I thought. *You've got to show total innocence! Don't even let yourself think anything except total innocence.*

"Huh?" I asked, trying my absolute best to look befuddled. Then, just for good measure, I added, "Nothing, Mom. Really. Everything was just fine."

"Don't you dare lie to me! And get that expression off your face before I wipe it off for you! I can tell just by looking at you that something isn't right! Now what happened at school?" she demanded.

It was all over. I knew it and finally blubbered out the truth. She had used her magic to read my mind again.

But she didn't only use it on me. She did it to my father too. When there were times I wanted something or wanted to do something I knew my father wouldn't go along with, I just naturally went to Mom. If I could pull it off with her, she'd eventually say, "All right, I'll see what I can do, but don't you say a word about it to your father. Just let me handle it."

Sure enough, we'd be sitting at dinner and my mom would casually skirt the subject, never hitting it dead on like I would have done. Although I just itched to jump in with my most magnificent sales pitch, I also knew from experience that I'd better keep my mouth shut.

With impeccable timing she'd glance at him a certain way and then reach over and ever so lightly touch his hand or shoulder for just the briefest second or so. After a few minutes, he'd start talking and eventually come up with an idea. Sure enough, "his idea" would be exactly what I had wanted!

More magic!

If you have children, you know how this "magic" works. If you're a mother, you know instinctively. By and large, while men can condition themselves with practice to the intricacies of nonverbal communication and persuasion, women come by it naturally, both receiving and transmitting, even if they are unaware of it at the time. Plus, they have what has often been mistakenly downplayed—women's intuition—a very real, very natural phenomenon thrown in for good measure.

Every day of our lives we are literally bombarded with images and impressions upon which we make instant decisions not necessarily having any basis whatsoever in logic or reason. Those impressions operate below our level of conscious awareness, influencing our behavior, thinking patterns, acceptance and rejection, ability to communicate, and the way we physically feel.

Most people are not aware that such an elaborate system even exists, some recognize its existence but don't know exactly how it works, and only a select few are knowledgeable or efficient at both *consciously transmitting* exactly what they desire or *consciously receiving* images and then *interpreting* them accurately.

This is the difference between the professional persuader who succeeds consistently by design and the amateur who succeeds every so often, mostly by accident. Once the amateur feels he is on track, he will charge ahead, completely oblivious to the reactions of his subjects, never varying or altering course but simply hoping for the best. If you've ever been in front of someone like this, you know what I mean. He's talking and you're bored, but out of pure courtesy you sit and continue to listen, wondering if this guy will ever shut up.

He, on the other hand, thinks that your sitting there indicates not only your interest but also agreement and he therefore continues, never bothering to read what you are telling him nonverbally, never even coming close to attracting your interest, much less persuading you of anything. Then at the end he wonders what happened.

The professional realizes that persuasion can only be successfully effected when matched to the specific motivators and stimulators of the subject. To accomplish this, he or she is constantly aware of what the subject is *really* saying both verbally and nonverbally. The professional has the ability to recognize when the subject is really in agreement, but, more importantly, when he is not; when the subject truly believes and understands the various aspects, but, more importantly, when he does not. The professional understands that signals and transmissions are being communicated in both directions on a continual basis and gauges the presentation accordingly.

And that's wherein lies the real difference.

"Nobility and dignity, self-abasement and servility, prudence and understanding, insolence and vulgarity are reflected in the face and attitudes of the body whether still or in motion."

—SOCRATES

Everything about you communicates something to someone. The words you use and your tone of voice (Chapter Five), your facial expression, the way you look at or avoid looking at someone, your handshake, gestures, posture, and the way you move are significant factors in determining exactly how people receive or reject you. Since only 40 percent of communication and therefore persuasion is verbal and 60 percent is accomplished by nonverbal associations, what you transmit to someone *nonverbally* has even more influence than what you actually say to them.

For example, have you ever known someone whom at first you didn't like, only to find that after a while, you really enjoyed their company? Ever seen someone you thought really seemed like a nice person even before meeting them? Have you ever met someone and been immediately "turned off" before even a word was spoken?

"I've never actually met the guy but from what I've seen, I wouldn't trust him around the corner!" or "She obviously really thinks she is somebody!" are examples of judgments people make every day based purely on negative nonverbal projection and interpretation, which may or may not be valid yet is the most effective and sometimes most devastating of all communication.

Visual Nonverbal Communication

An interesting story which illustrates this is about a sweet little Jewish lady walking down the street in the Bronx carrying her groceries home. Suddenly a flasher leaps in front of her from an alley and spreads his trench coat, revealing his naked body. Calmly she looks from one side of his coat to the other, smiles critically, and says, "Ha! And you call *that* a quality lining?"

In this case, what the flasher was intent upon showing her was not what she was seeing, or at least what she chose to see.

The greatest majority of nonverbal communication is visual primarily because we live in a visually oriented society. Studies reveal that nearly 98 percent of people surveyed would, forced to make the choice, rather be deaf than blind. That's why television commercials are generally more effective than print and radio combined.

MTV, for example, which was originally predicted to be a failure by network "experts" who had little understanding of the power of combining both visual and audio subliminal persuasion, has skyrocketed in ratings and in millions of dollars in the sale of commercial time. The reason it has been so successful is that it virtually eliminates the need for any creative or independent thought on the part of the viewer. Combining words, music, visuals, and in some cases a rhythmic, almost hypnotic beat, music videos feed very specific messages directly into not only the conscious but, more importantly, the subliminal mind of the viewer. While some messages may be bold and open, those which are more subtle and hardly detectable are by far the most effective and influential, as you will soon understand.

One needn't use one's imagination to realize the potential

power this medium could wield in the wrong hands, much less the damage it has already done or its contribution to ongoing societal problems. But that's a completely separate subject.

Another marketing failure predicted by the "experts" was the video recorder and player. This opinion was based on the assumption that the majority of the American public would find them too complicated to program. What they failed to consider, however, was the market's appeal to the visual stimulus and flexibility offered by the units, if only for the purpose of renting and playing movies not offered by the networks. The result: today expensive VCRs are outselling new TVs.

Visual communication and especially persuasion are not, however, limited strictly to what we can see. In some cases, it is even more effective when *not* seen.

Subliminal Persuasion: A Deceptive Practice?

In the late sixties and early seventies, moviegoers suddenly began flocking to concession counters to purchase popcorn, soda, candy, and chocolate bars in record numbers. Sales and profits from the movie stands skyrocketed and rumors of mysterious origins began to surface, eventually prompting an investigation into the unexplained cause of "cravings" people felt suddenly and for no apparent reason.

The investigation resulted in findings that some theater owners were splicing frames of popcorn, candy, and soft drinks into and throughout the movies. On the screen for only a fraction of a second, the messages were unseen consciously by people engrossed in the movie, but easily picked up by their subconscious minds, causing them to crave products sold at the concession stands. In fact, this method was so powerful as a mind and behavior modification vehicle that it even caused viewers to prefer one brand over another.

Once this was discovered, legislation was introduced to prevent its use on the basis that it was too effective in literally forcing people to buy products without their conscious consent. Shortly thereafter, this technology came to be known as subliminal advertising. Following a 1984 investigation, the Bureau of Alcohol, Tobacco and Firearms supported the prohibition of subliminal inserts (imbeds) in the advertising of alcoholic beverages, an action which the FCC had already supported and prohibited by regulation.

But even though legislation prevented the use of subliminal imbeds, advertisers and agencies, realizing the power of subliminal advertising, immediately began to look for other ways to accomplish the same results without specifically violating the law. Today, through advanced technology, subliminal advertising has been substantially improved and billions of dollars are spent on its use to legally advertise a wide variety of products. Among some of the more noticeable are beer, perfume, automobile, travel, aftershave, and fitness conditioning commercials, where a fine line is drawn between "subliminal" by definition and "subliminal" by effect.

What, for example, are they really selling in the beer commercial? In a series of quick cuts they typically show a party on the beach, in a bar, or at a picnic with beautiful people enjoying the atmosphere, warmth, and each other's friendship. Are they really selling beer? Do the commercials emphasize the beer's color, taste, or flavor as they did years ago? Or are they instead persuading you that if you drink this beer, you too can be popular, attractive, and part of that special in-crowd?

Does the fitness spa commercial really sell health? Or does it instead show superattractive Venuses and Adonises helping each other work out, a glistening sheen of sweat covering and highlighting their bodies? As the camera zooms into areas you would be embarrassed to be caught looking at, what do you think is really being sold?

When was the last time you saw a perfume or after-shave commercial emphasizing a pleasant scent? That doesn't sell perfume or aftershave.

What does sell is the subliminal implication that when you wear it, you'll be absolutely irresistible to the opposite sex, "wearing this, or nothing at all."

The effective use of subliminal persuasion is not, however, limited to video mediums. It is also widely used in print advertising and packaging. In almost every example of subliminal techniques it is important to notice that while ads use both photographs and artwork, agencies and advertisers will more often spend literally hundreds of times the cost of a photograph to instead use a painted representation. The reason for this is that the subliminal can be imbedded in the painting in a much more subtle, cost-efficient, and effective presentation than in a photograph.

Interestingly enough, while visual subliminals of all types may not be realized consciously, the results of their impressions are recorded and evidence of their effect is documented in EKGs, EEGs, and GSRs (galvanic skin response tests). In fact, research also reveals that the deeper and less obvious the subliminal, the more potent its effect. Based upon this, someone is undoubtedly going to say that nonverbal, subliminal communication and persuasion is wrong because it can be used to manipulate, confuse, deceive, and even coerce without the subject's knowledge or awareness.

True. But so do words, agreements, contracts, and even conversation.

The fact of the matter is that we are *already and on a daily basis* both transmitting and receiving nonverbal subliminal communication and persuasion. Unfortunately, most of the time the majority of people are not consciously aware of it, nor are they aware of precisely what is being communicated, which puts them at a disadvantage.

When properly understood and applied, its use is a positive and a definite asset, not only to you but to everyone with whom you are associated.

In addition to providing you with the ability to communicate precisely what you mean with crystal clarity to avoid the possibility of confusion and misunderstanding, it helps you to put others at ease, to "read" their nonverbal communication to determine how and if they are receptive to what you are saying, to decide whether to proceed faster or more slowly, and to identify the points on which they agree or disagree.

By being aware of precisely what you are communicating nonverbally, you more efficiently project the image you desire, effecting better communication by reinforcing nonverbally what you are communicating verbally.

An awareness of nonverbal interpretation also enables you to "read" how people are responding to what you are saying and alerts you to changes or adjustments you have to make to result in better communication and comprehension.

By being more competent and precise in nonverbal communication and persuasion skills, you not only develop self-confidence in both your business and personal life, but you avoid the confusion and misunderstandings which often and needlessly ruin good relationships.

And finally, it eliminates the possibility of unconsciously being dominated by others.

It is, however, a language of its own and can only be grasped and its vocabulary expanded with practice.

For openers, let's take a look at nonverbal communication which either complements and reinforces or completely contradicts and invalidates what you express verbally.

The First Impression

Everyone knows that the first impression is important. In fact, every salesperson has heard it said that the sale is made or lost within the first few minutes of meeting a prospect.

Unfortunately, it's also a primary concept most people forget. "People shouldn't judge a person by the way they look. It's what's inside that counts. There's no reason in the world I shouldn't wear clothes or styles I like just because someone might be offended by my appearance," is a common statement especially by those who enjoy being different or in some way separating themselves from the majority.

And it's true. People should not be judged on appearances alone. But the words *should* and *should not* have nothing to do with the real world, where everyone is in the business of persuasion.

The Eyes of the Beholder

A rock star wearing a three-piece suit, conservative hairstyle and behaving in a businesslike manner would have about as much success impressing groupies at a concert as a corporate attorney trying to influence a board of directors while wearing his hair to the waist, sporting outlandish earrings, and acting as if he were high on drugs.

A major part of persuasion is an appearance conforming to the expectations of the majority to whom it is being directed, the key word being *majority*.

While dressing outlandishly and wearing gaudy jewelry or hairstyles may appeal to a fractional minority, you increase your success in life by persuading as many people as possible. And unless you know your subject intimately, the general rule to follow is neutrality with good taste as it applies to situations and people.

Even before a formal introduction, the conscious and subconscious minds of both you and your subject(s) are bombarded with impressions which will be critically important to communication. This is the point of initial acceptance or rejection on both sides, which will predominate consciously and subconsciously throughout the discussion and be extremely difficult to change.

In sales, for example, the most widely accepted appearance

for a man is clean shaven. While mustaches are generally acceptable, beards and longer-than-average hair are a definite disadvantage. Clothing, hairstyles, and shoes should be conservative and neat.

Another important consideration must be given to gender differences. For women, conservative but stylish hairdos and a minimum of makeup combined with apparel to fit the occasion is a good rule to follow. Extreme care must especially be taken when women are dealing with other women because women tend to be more sensitive to and critical of the style and makeup of other women than men would be of another man.

Men tend to formulate a visual impression within the first seven to twenty seconds, forming a judgment strictly on the physical appearance of either a man or woman, and then make a second judgment within the following one to two minutes which combines physical appearance, handshake, and general personality.

Women, on the other hand, tend to be more conservative, do not place as much immediate emphasis on a physical judgment, and establish their initial impression within the first two minutes of meeting someone. Their first impression is likely to be based primarily on their "feelings" (women's intuition) toward that individual, either male or female, but with an inclination to be much more critical in the case of women, where makeup and dress come into play.

Regardless of gender, however, the initial impression created within this time frame tends to last throughout the first meeting and, while it may be modified somewhat, is generally difficult if not impossible to change completely.

Adding Color to Your Presentation

Do you always want to be dressed in the most fashionable color? Is color important in relating to the season of the year, your particular skin tones, or the shade of your eyes? Are you especially comfortable in a certain color or feel you look best in that color?

Everyone has personal preferences when it comes to color. But if persuasion and achieving the best possible effect and least resistance in the shortest period of time possible are a consideration, color preferences may have to be modified, at least in business situations.

Most important is the awareness that all single-tone colors have both positive and negative connotations. For example:

Red is bold, aggressive, extroverted, and exciting, but it also represents anger, danger, sin, and blood.

Blue, associated with loyalty, truth, and serenity, is also pleasant, cool, and modest. It can, however, convey sadness and discouragement.

Yellow, while bright and cheery, can also be hostile, cowardly, and diseased.

Green is peaceful and calm, fresh, youthful, and prosperous. But it also relates to envy and inexperience.

Orange is lively and bright but can be irritating, noisy, and unpleasant.

Purple is stately and passionate, but is also aloof and tends to imply authority and dominance.

White is innocence, purity, and cleanliness. On the other hand, it can also be seen as plain and cold.

Black, while ultraconservative and businesslike, is also viewed as villainous, desperate, wicked, and futile.

So what is the answer?

As a general rule, stay away from the solid colors. Instead, wear subtle tones in combination for the most neutral effect if the type of person you expect to be persuading falls into an average or general category. At the other end of the spectrum, if you're dealing with a rock or heavy metal musician, the sky's the limit and you'd fit in looking like a rainbow.

Dollars and Scents

One of the most instantaneous of all subconscious and subliminal triggers is our olfactory system. Scents are very powerful stimuli, quickly and subliminally recalling memories, feelings, and emotions both pleasant and unpleasant.

How many people instantly remember their childhood with the first smell of a freshly mown lawn? How does the smell of a farm bring back memories to those who, twenty, thirty, forty, or even fifty years ago were raised in that environment?

On an unpleasant note, what about the wife who discovers her husband has been seeing another woman by noticing the odor of the girlfriend's perfume on his shirt? What do you suppose would be her conscious and/or subconscious reaction to smelling a similar perfume on another woman?

To make it even more complicated, after-shave, cologne, perfume, and deodorants may appeal to one person and be repulsive to another. Hairsprays, for example, while smelling pleasant to you, may have the unique property of sending someone else into fits of sneezing. And although a scent worn by one person may be pleasant, it could very easily smell completely different on another due to their chemical makeup.

The best general rule is to use unscented deodorants and avoid after-shave, perfume, cologne, and hairsprays altogether if possible. If for some reason a hairspray is necessary, opt for the unscented variety.

Smokers have yet another challenge, pipe and cigar smokers even more. While they are not particularly aware of it, smoke and the smell of smoke permeates clothes, hair, and breath and is especially noticeable, usually repugnant, and a definite negative influence on the first impression on nonsmokers.

While the obvious solution would be to quit smoking completely, that option is easier said than done. As a secondary alternative, smokers should make sure to have their clothes cleaned often, shampoo daily, and immediately prior to a persuasion situation avoid smoking. It would also be prudent to use the variety of breath sprays, drops, and mouthwashes on the market whether smokers think they need them or not. (They always do.) These alternatives, while not a solution to the problem, at least soften it.

Posturing for Effect

Posture and the way a person moves also weighs heavily on the first impression, as well as throughout the entire encounter, and is one of the most subliminal of all factors upon which people make assessments.

At first glance, a viewer determines sometimes consciously but *always subconsciously* whether someone is confident and poised, relaxed or stressed, friendly or aloof, ambitious or lack-adaisical. Posture and movement transmit feelings about the encounter, but more importantly also reflect feelings of self-esteem, ambition, drive, confidence, and ability. Does the person have a confident stride and lively gait, or simply shuffle from one place to another? Stand straight but relaxed, rigid and in-flexible, or slouch and fidget?

Posture, movement, and overall physiology also communicate someone's moods and emotions.

For example, how would you stand if you were absolutely elated, confident, and proud of yourself? Your head would be up, a smile on your face, and you'd walk with a bounce in your step. Life is absolutely wonderful and it would show.

Now how would you stand if you were depressed, worried about not being able to pay your bills, knowing that your wife, kids, and even the dog hated to see you come home? Your face would wear a frown, you'd probably be slumped or slouched over, and even slow walking would be an effort.

If you want an interesting experiment, try switching moods and postures. Stand tall, proud, and smiling and try to be de-pressed. Now slump over, put a frown on your face, and shuf-fle around trying to be happy.

It simply doesn't work, does it? So if you want to change your mood, change your physiology. The important thing to keep in mind is that posture not only tells you about someone else, it tells them about you.

Putting Your Best Foot Forward

The way you move toward and with a person forms impressions in their subconscious, not only about you as an individual but also about your attitude and approach to the encounter with them. If you are slouched and shuffle toward and with them, that is the judgment they form of you as a person—one who tends to be sloppy and lacks confidence, initiative, and probably competence. Additionally, this posture and movement may indicate to them that you place little importance on and in fact may even be bored with them, more or less going through the motions because it's required of you. At the opposite extreme, if you move in a quick, agitated gait, your subjects may attribute this also to lack of confidence, nervousness, and possibly even deception.

Reading this, you might well counter by saying that those are unfair and illogical judgments based strictly upon the way a person walks.

Be reminded again: **Unconscious, subliminal impressions are not necessarily—and in fact most often are not—based upon reason or logic. Nonetheless, they have a devastating effect in any persuasion situation. The words** *fair* **or** *unfair* **have no application when dealing with the subconscious.**

Whenever you walk into a room and especially into the presence of people you are meeting for the first time, think of yourself as owning the place instead of just being there as another guest. Concentrate on straight but not rigid posture and an easy and deliberate gait. Look around the room, acknowledging people with a relaxed expression and moderate smile.

A nod of recognition, even to people you've not yet met, works wonders when you are eventually introduced to them.

Standing Tall

The same general characteristics and the impressions people form based upon the way you move also apply to the way you stand.

If you're slouched over, fidget, and look like you've just recently acquired a pair of arms and hands that you're not quite sure what to do with yet, it will convey the glaring impression that you're probably nervous, lack confidence, and may even be incompetent.

On the other hand, if you stand as if you have a steel rod jammed up your backside and your arms are folded across your chest or hidden behind your back, you'll appear intimidating and aggressive, giving the impression that your secret goal in life is to be a prison warden or commanding officer of a military base.

Relax! Stand tall, not rigid, as if you are introducing yourself to people who are visiting you in your home. Let your arms hang loosely at your sides or put them in the same position as those of the people you are meeting. Keep in mind that they're coming to see you, not the other way around.

"Put 'Er There!"

The initial handshake, while lasting only seconds, also blasts the subliminal with impressions critically important to communication and ultimate persuasion.

The first consideration is whether a handshake is even warranted or acceptable. There are people of both genders who simply *do not want to be touched* by a stranger even in a gesture as socially acceptable as a handshake. While they will tolerate it in a social, business, selling, or persuasion situation, they do so only because they feel forced into it.

Again, there is a gender difference. Even in the case of people who do not like to be touched, a woman can usually offer a handshake to either a man or another woman without difficulty. A man can usually get away with it with another man. But the most extreme care must be taken on the part of a man offering to shake a woman's hand, and when done, it should be very brief.

Ideally, with people of this nature, you would have a distinct advantage forgoing the handshake altogether and instead allowing your subject(s) to warm up to you before touching of any kind proceeds, if at all.

If you happen to be a person who is not particularly into touching and have ever visited a car dealership, you already know exactly what I mean. As you're browsing through the rows of cars you look toward the office and see the line of salespeople shuffling back and forth. Suddenly, one of them looks in your direction and the entire group snaps to attention as the next "up" salesperson slides in your direction. Once he is within ten to fifteen feet away, the facial expression changes. A huge smile lights up his face and he immediately extends his hand as he advances on your position. Sound military? It is.

"Hey, how ya doin'? My name is Jack Sellingallatime. I'll bet you're looking for a good deal, right?" he says as he grabs your hand and squeezes with all his might in a bone-crushing grip because the sales manager has told him everybody respects a rock-hard handshake.

If you've ever had that happen, you know how irritating it is, and I'm not even a person who is normally averse to shaking hands. Someone who doesn't like to be touched would be completely put off by it and the road to a sale could be rocky and long.

In this case, a much better alternative for the salesperson would be starting the conversation with something other than an introduction. He could ask if there were anything in particular the subject might be looking for. After learning that, he could then use a "By the way, my name is . . . and you are—?" introduction, slightly lifting his hand as if to begin the gesture. If the subject responds, then by all means he should proceed with the handshake. If not, he would be wise to instead verbalize his pleasure at meeting them, etc., etc.

When a handshake is initiated, a number of factors come into play. A soft or rough, moist or dry skin texture; a crushing, firm, or flimsy handshake; and the duration it is held—all create lasting impressions. The texture of a woman's hand is expected to be soft. If the texture of a man's hand is soft, however, another man, and some women, tend to respond negatively. Another negative is a moist and somewhat cold (clammy) handshake, which subliminally reveals anxiety or stress. At both the conscious and subconscious levels, this is an immediate turnoff to everyone.

The pressure of a handshake, both given and received, also establishes subliminal impressions. The person (usually a man) who spends his off hours squeezing tennis balls to develop his grip wants to show everyone how strong he is and often uses the same grip with women as with men. Subliminally he's telegraphing aggressiveness and a desire to dominate, which in most cases is received negatively. If done with a man of the same inclinations, this handshake results in each attempting to inconspicuously subjugate the other, not only with the handshake but also with mutual "power stares" (covered later in this book).

It shouldn't be difficult to understand that this "contest of wills" will also be carried into any persuasion situation, making it difficult if not impossible.

The best handshake is one of moderation, to learn the intentions of the other. If the pressure of the handshake is matched, it signals a spirit of cooperation. If the pressure is suddenly reduced, it indicates submissiveness.

If you find yourself in the clutches of Gregor the Grip, however, you already know what you're dealing with and the important thing here is to finish the handshake without allowing him to feel he has dominated. Returning the grip will only result in an Indian wrestling match which will end up negatively regardless of who wins. The simple solution is to maintain a firm grip while smiling and immediately taking one step toward him. This sudden invasion of space will literally throw him off center, his grip will relax, and at that point you release the handshake, ending the contest before it has a chance to begin.

Another subliminal indicator of intention during a handshake is the position of the hands. A person who offers his or her hand palm down shows their immediate desire to dominate. The hand offered vertically with the thumb up indicates a cooperative, open attitude, while the hand offered palm up indicates a tendency toward submissiveness, subservience, and subordination.

Some people like to use both hands in the process of a hand-shake. While this is effective when meeting acquaintances and as a farewell in establishing a warm, lasting friendship, it should never be used during an introduction because it subliminally conveys what might be received as a phony attempt at warmth. And especially in the case of a person who does not appreciate being touched, it should be avoided completely.

Once a relationship and rapport have been established, however, there are primarily two styles of two-handed hand-shake, both of which are effective because they allow you to enter and share the other person's "space zone" without invading it.

The enclosing handshake consists of holding the other person's hand with both of yours. Used without any up-and-down motion, it conveys that you are extending safety and security as a result of their decision to agree with you. It also transmits feelings that you have a personal relationship with them and are interested in their well-being.

The other two-hander consists of shaking hands in the normal manner while grasping any part of the person's right arm with your left hand. Another form of reassurance, this method basically says, "You've made the right decision and I'll look out for your best interests." Be aware, however, that the higher up you move your left hand, the more you are invading their space and therefore, the more rapport you must have with that person to avoid causing any discomfort.

The duration of the handshake is also important. While the average handshake lasts about three seconds, anything longer initiated by the other person generally indicates interest, a willingness to cooperate, and openness to touching. Held too long, however, the person will quickly begin to feel trapped and even agitated.

The most important aspect of the handshake in general is to be aware of exactly what is happening throughout its duration. While most people unconsciously or absentmindedly perform this function as a ritual, it can provide a wealth of information for those who are alert to its intricacies in any persuasion situation.

A "Touchy" Subject

Characteristics and general rules applying to the handshake also extend to touching subjects during the persuasion process.

Again, if dealing with a person who does not like to be touched, any physical contact is an immediate turnoff, causing antagonism, embarrassment, and even rejection.

When done properly, however, under the right circumstances and with the right people, limited touching is extremely effective in putting people at ease, making them receptive, and providing reassurance. Primary zones of concentration include brief touches on the shoulders, forearms, and hands, used when agreeing with the subject or to emphasize a certain point.

Again, there is a gender variation. While men are usually and relatively comfortable being touched by a woman regardless of the level of familiarity, they are seldom receptive to being touched by other men. Women, although they generally and frequently touch and hug other female and male friends and are comfortable being touched, can have a disagreeable reaction to being touched by an unfamiliar male.

As a general rule, therefore, men should avoid touching either men or women. Women, on the other hand, can be more flexible, touching either men or women as long as the touches are brief and confined to the hands, shoulders, and forearms.

Positioning for Persuasion

The position of your body while in a discussion with one or more people also has a bearing on how well you will be able to communicate and persuade, again with an important gender difference.

For the most part, men tend to position themselves directly in front of someone they know and like. When first meeting a stranger, however, this position can cause subliminal confrontation, antagonism, or even hostility. Therefore, if you are a man, it is generally more acceptable when first meeting another male to position yourself at a slight angle. Women, on the other hand, tend to prefer adjacent positions when talking to friends and fond acquaintances. When meeting strangers, however, they prefer to be directly facing them.

An exception to these situations occurs when a male or female is in a persuasion situation with an unfamiliar couple. In the case of a female, it is always wise to be directly adjacent to the other female and either across from or at an angle to her male counterpart. A male, however, will be more effective closer and at an angle to the other male and directly facing his female counterpart.

Similar rules apply in a seated position. The most important thing to remember is that unless it is your intention to make someone feel subservient or intimidated, in which case you will risk hostility or even an aggressive response, never discuss anything if you are standing and they are seated. Also keep in mind that the more a person begins to be receptive to you, the closer they will move, be it leaning over a table or moving closer in a standing position. The less receptive they are, the more they will move away from you. Both of these responses are purely subliminal and will vary during the conversation.

Being aware of movements, therefore, gives you an obvious advantage in gauging how fast or slowly to proceed, what is readily acceptable, and what is not.

"*I Need My Space, Man!*"

Trite, but true.

Proxemics, which is the study of the way people use their own personal space to communicate, tells us that every person sets up a "safety zone" around themselves and that the size of that zone depends upon the individual, the relationship to the people around them, and the type of meeting which is to take place.

Regardless of the size or distance this zone encompasses, intrusion into it has been proven to cause not only psychological changes but also physiological increases in heart rate, blood pressure, and muscle tension. These factors will invariably affect both the tone and outcome of the discussion or relationship. Intrusion into a person's zone creates an impression of dominance, intimidation, and aggression. Too much distance, conversely, implies an aloof, cold, or disinterested attitude.

As a general rule, zero to two feet is considered an intimate zone, two to four feet the personal zone, and five feet or more the public zone.

Although everyone is different with regard to their personal comfort zones, there do exist some interesting generalities in ethnic categories. Arabs, Japanese, South Americans, French, Greeks, Black North Americans, Italians, and Spaniards tend to prefer a rather close zone. Britons, Swedes, Swiss, Germans, and Austrians generally prefer a moderate zone. White North Americans, Orientals, Australians, and New Zealanders have a tendency toward a distant zone.

Once the basis of a relationship is established, moving inside a person's comfort zone can actually increase their receptivity. However, caution is the watchword and timing a main consideration. If you have misconstrued their response and they are not properly prepared or ready for this type of move, you may create an attitude or reaction which will actually be detrimental to your purpose. Reestablishing the relationship will then be much more difficult and time consuming.

The best practice is to be aware of the person's movements, allowing them to establish their own comfort zone. As time passes and they become more receptive, you will notice them moving within closer proximity to you. At that point, you can begin moving closer to them. If you notice them backing away, do the same. If they move even closer, allow it to happen with the realization that you are in the process of successful persuasion.

Let's Face It!

Every person in the world has a very special and unique identity, personality, and temperament, which could not be more effectively communicated than by their own face.

While physiologists estimate that people are capable of over twenty thousand different facial expressions in both voluntary and involuntary muscles, most people are not satisfied with their natural appearance. Instead, they modify it with cosmetic, physical, and even surgical changes—some to appear what they consider more attractive, younger, or older, more serious or less serious, more physically fit and active; some to better express what they feel is their identity, or on the opposite side of the coin, to hide or change their identity; and some, simply for fun and variety.

Different social customs and cultures also cause people to paint, mutilate, deform, tattoo, scar, mask, reshape, and transform their faces to change their identity in keeping with their personal status.

Yet for all the physical transformations, facial expressions continue to reveal thoughts, intentions, and moods more accurately than words. While everyone uses and can identify these expressions, few actually pay enough attention to them whether on another person or themselves.

Concentrating on what feelings they transmit, however, gives you an incredible advantage in evaluating how the other person is receiving your message, their level of belief in what you are saying, when they question or agree with you, and a multitude of other responses. Most important to keep in mind is that their facial movements are actually communicating what they are thinking at the time. And it is equally crucial that you pay attention to your own expressions, making sure that what you are saying with your voice is being confirmed on your face.

The Eyebrow Twitch

Prior to an actual introduction, you often "meet" people with a glance before a word is ever exchanged. The very first impression formed is based upon the eyes, mouth, and facial expression.

One way to determine the receptivity of a person in an actual introduction is to display a moderate smile and an "eyebrow twitch," which is the movement of one or both eyebrows about a fifth of a second in duration. If your subject stares in return, lifts the head and lowers the eyelids, or simply averts their gaze, the meeting may be off to a bad start, but at least you have an indication of the attitude with which you will be dealing.

If the person simply stares at you, refusing to return the twitch, this is an indication that they are "all business." On the other hand, if they smile and return the twitch, you're off to a good start.

When using this technique, care should be taken that it occurs six to ten feet apart. If you are farther than that apart, they may not see it. On the other hand, if you are within five feet, it might strike them that something is wrong or that you are surprised or even disappointed.

The Eyes Have It

Was there ever a parent who did not communicate with their children simply by looking at them a certain way? I know both of mine did!

When I was a child, if we were out in public and I started acting up, both my mother and father had a very special and unique way of communicating to me, without ever saying a word, "Just keep it up and see what happens!" How many have ever heard a parent say, "Don't you dare look at me that way!"

Communication and persuasion often depend on how you use your eyes. Initial eye contact with someone you are just meeting should be intense but brief, **never** more than three to five seconds. Anything more than that can be subliminally interpreted as hostile, challenging, or intimidating, even if the other person is not consciously receiving those signals. After the initial three to five seconds, the contact should be broken with a quick sideways glance, never downward, as that would imply servility, passivity, or even deception.

During conversation, a good general rule is to look with fairly long glances while listening, and less while talking. Look away when you take control of the conversation; look back when turning it over.

The mood you want to create also depends on the use of your eyes in conjunction with your expression. If warmth and goodwill are your intention, look with a soft smile. On the other hand, should you desire to intimidate, show aggression, or challenge a person, a long, unsmiling stare will usually accomplish that goal quite easily. This is the one responsible for the expression "If looks could kill."

The concept of staring as a sign of aggression, by the way, is not limited exclusively to humans. It exists in almost all species of mammals, for whom long staring usually initiates a challenge. The receiver of the stare most often has only one of two alternatives: to back off and give way, or accept the challenge and attack.

An interesting illustration for the more courageous would be to walk past a Doberman or German Shepherd either in a kennel or with its master. Usually, there will be only a slightly aggressive response, if any. Now, instead of simply walking past, stop and stare directly into the animal's eyes and see what happens. (Incidentally, I accept no responsibility or liability for the outcome of this experiment.)

The eyes are more than a mirror to the soul, they are also a mirror of what is going on in the mind. As a result, your ability to persuade also depends on how accurately you "read" what the other person is saying with their eyes. If, while you are speaking, the person is looking directly at you with both eyes wide open, keep going, as it indicates a desire on their part to know more. If, at some time during your part of the conversation, the person begins to squint slightly, you are in an area in which they have either a question or doubt about whatever you're discussing. This is a warning sign. If you continue, they may not question you, but be assured they've made a mental note which will impede persuasion later in the conversation.

At this point, the best thing to do is stop immediately! Question what their feelings are about the point, or ask if they completely understand what you're saying to get the matter cleared up before continuing.

Let's say that while you're talking, the person seems to be glancing to one or the other side. This indicates stress of some kind which is either self-induced or caused by you. In either case, if you continue under these circumstances, you'll accomplish little. Again, confront the problem head-on, with a casual comment that they seem to be nervous about something, and simply ask if they might be more comfortable in a different setting.

If the person's head is tilted forward and the eyes are looking directly at you under the upper eyelids, watch out! This one says they not only disbelieve you, but you're in for a fight! So be prepared, because a confrontation is definitely on the way.

Gender Differences

Effective eye contact also differs depending upon the genders involved. In man-to-man or woman-to-woman conversations, eye contact should ideally be maintained about 70 percent of the time. More is considered intrusive and intimidating, while less is considered shifty. In conversations between a woman and a man, however, 50 percent is generally more acceptable.

Where to Look

In a business situation, your gaze should be fixed within the triangle formed across the top of the eyes to the tip of the nose. This conveys not only self-confidence but a genuine interest in the person.

In social situations, your gaze should take in a much larger spectrum, across the top of the eyes to the point of the chin.

This conveys not only a more intimate interest in the person but also a desire to know them better.

When to Look

Always immediately look at the person who starts talking. It conveys interest in what they're saying. Break contact at any pause in their speech and look back again when they begin.

Also break contact before you begin to speak. When you start, reestablish contact and when you finish, glance away. If you expect a response, glance toward them.

Grading the Pupil

The pupil is one of the most sensitive and intricate parts of the body, very similar to the lens opening of a camera reacting to different intensities of light. But more importantly, it also re-acts to emotion.

As a result, correctly evaluating its changes is one of the least known yet most effective, scientifically documented techniques to accurately gauge a person's response to what you are saying because it is completely involuntary and out of the control of the subject, virtually eliminating the possibility of purposeful deception.

Simply put, when a person is aroused, interested, and re-ceptive to something, the pupils dilate. Physically, this is an at-tempt on the part of the eye to allow more light to enter even though the amount of light in the surrounding area remains the same.

In fact, and subliminally, it is an attempt to allow the entry of more information. Accompanying the pupil dilation, you will also generally notice increased frequency of eye contact, frequent head movements, and positional movements toward you.

When the pupils contract, however, usually with a decrease in frequency of eye contact, this is conversely an indication that the person is not receptive, does not want to hear what is being said, and is in a rejection mode.

So accurate is this method of gauging acceptance and rejection that highly sophisticated market research companies often install hidden microprocessor-based photographic equipment in retail outlets. These cameras actually measure individual pupil dilation and contraction for the purpose of measuring positive and negative response as shoppers glance at different packaging.

If you are presenting a product, idea, or perhaps yourself to another person, noticing the pupil response of your subject is therefore an excellent method of determining your direction, speed, acceptance, or rejection.

Shifty Eyes

Evasive eyes are *sometimes* a sign of deceit. The syndrome includes nervously avoiding eye contact for extended periods, refusing to make any direct eye contact, and even closing the eyes momentarily during conversation.

Notice the word *sometimes,* because assuming any generality here could be a disastrous mistake in the persuasion process. For example, to assume that people who do not have shifty eyes are completely honest and forthright would be incorrect. In fact, the more dishonest someone is, and the more practiced at deception, the more they are usually aware of the opinion people have of shifty eyes. Knowing this, they concentrate heavily on maintaining direct eye contact against their natural tendency to do otherwise.

Evasive eyes might also merely indicate that the person is nervous, under some kind of strain or pressure, shy, agitated, anxious, or simply has no interest in whatever it is you are saying. By the same token, it is not altogether inconceivable that you might be the source of their nervousness by invading their comfort zone with too much eye contact during the initial part of the conversation.

As stated previously, the first remedy would be to simply ask if they are uncomfortable or would prefer a different setting for the discussion. Next, reduce the amount of eye contact, only gradually increasing it as you notice signs of anxiety lessening. As you do so, make sure to add a warm smile and perhaps a compliment to put them even more at ease.

While it is impossible to make any generalities about shifty eyes, it is important and in fact an advantage to keep all the possibilities in mind when speaking to someone who has this trait to be able to use it to your advantage. It is also just as important to remember if you happen to be the one who is nervous during a conversation to concentrate on your own eye movement, thereby avoiding the possibility of being misjudged.

"Cool Shades, Man!"

The subject of eye contact would not be complete without mentioning the use of sunglasses and, for that matter, tinted eyeglasses. While a number of people jump to the defense of both, it's only because they wear them.

In fact, in a persuasion situation, subjects automatically distrust a person wearing sunglasses, sometimes consciously but always subconsciously, with the assumption that use of the glasses is a direct attempt to hide the eyes in fear that they will reveal the truth.

"Yeah, but I only wear them when I go outside. Never in the office," is the common excuse.

Fine. While you're outside speaking to people face-to-face or simply looking in another direction, are your eyes cold and calculating? Are they shifting back and forth as you try to think up different approaches to persuade them? Are they squinting in the formation of devious plans?

"Heck no! My eyes are the same as they were when I met the people and first talked to them. They should know that!"

Really? How should they know that?

Simply stated, if people cannot see your eyes clearly throughout *the entire process of persuasion,* they have the automatic inclination to assume the worst, thereby destroying any ground you may have gained to that point, regardless of whether you are looking at or away from them while wearing the glasses.

Assuming the statistics are way off, is being comfortable in tinted glasses or sunglasses worth losing even one in ten persuasion situations?

When You're Smiling, the Whole World Smiles with You

Smiling can put people at ease and conveys a friendly personality—but whatever you do, **don't overdo it,** especially when first meeting someone.

Remember, you have no idea of the type of personality with which you are dealing. Depending on their environment or geographic origin and orientation, your subject may take a big shining smile as friendly, phony, hostile, deceitful, intimidating, or challenging. So it's important to know something about this facial expression.

Smiles fall into three categories.

The low-intensity smile. This is perfectly acceptable during a conversation, especially when accompanied by a tilting of the head to convey friendliness and interest. Used during an introduction, however, it tends to indicate uncertainty and lack of confidence.

The moderate-intensity smile. Best used when meeting new people, this smile conveys an open, cooperative attitude and interest, especially when accompanied by the proper approach, stance, and body positioning.

The high-intensity smile. This should be reserved strictly for people with whom you have established a relationship or rapport. If done when first meeting people, it can imply a phony attempt to be personal and result in creating distrust.

The same goes for facial expression. Too radical an expression or one that appears frozen in place can be interpreted as deceitful, even hostile. On the other side of the coin, lack of expression while speaking tends to convey disinterest. Therefore, the best policy to follow in smiling and expression is one of moderation, at least until you become familiar with the subject who will, by their own features, set the limits.

The Mouth

The mouth communicates in many ways other than simply forming and projecting words. By its positioning and physical changes it can express everything from anger, hostility, fear, joy, confusion, and frustration to sexual arousal, when the lips become slightly swollen, darker in color, and more sensitive to touch.

Regardless of race, national origin, or environment, slightly opening the mouth is a universal sign of curiosity and interest. As the interest grows, the mouth will open more, even if only slightly. Conversely, a mouth which is clamped shut tells you that you are not getting through or that your subject is refusing to allow you to get through.

Here again, it is important to remember that your subject, like you, is consciously or subconsciously picking up the subliminal signals transmitted. When listening to what they are saying, be sure to face them with your mouth slightly open to indicate interest and receptivity to their part of the discussion.

A Cheeky Subject

Cheeks, like the dilation of the pupils, also respond involuntarily to stimulus and signal a variety of emotions. This is the area of the body which shows shame, embarrassment, and self-consciousness as blood rushes to the surface of the skin in what is commonly termed a blush. If a person becomes extremely agitated, hostile, antagonistic, and aggressive, the cheeks pale as blood drains in preparation for what might become a physical confrontation. The same physical changes result when a person becomes frightened or nervous. In both cases, the body instinctively prepares itself for the unknown.

While it is difficult if not impossible to control this physical response in yourself, being aware of it in the other person will give you an advantage.

Getting the Point

A lot of people in a persuasion situation prefer to use written presentation materials, including charts, graphs, and so on. Unfortunately this reduces eye contact and the advantages of gestures from 80 percent to less than 10 percent.

The first mistake most make when doing this is looking at the pages, numbers, and graphs at which they are pointing. How many would be surprised to suddenly look up and see their subject absentmindedly glancing around the room while they are the only ones intent on the pages? Instead, know your material well enough to be able to look at the subjects across the table or desk while pointing out whatever you might be illustrating on the page.

Ross Perot demonstrated his expertise in the use of printed materials during his famous infomercials. Even though he pointed to the charts and graphs, his eyes were in direct contact with the cameras during the majority of the presentation.

In a one-on-one presentation, this accomplishes two things. First, it makes your subject(s) aware that you are watching them to be sure their attention is drawn to the materials. Second, it gives you the opportunity to watch them for nonverbal signals they may display as they see certain information, most especially pupil dilation, as discussed previously. The very act of pointing also creates a variety of subliminal impressions.

Just for a moment, stop and think about how many ways there are to point to something or at someone to convey a multitude of impressions.

The variety is so numerous that an entire chapter could be devoted to this subject alone. The hand might be formed into a fist with only the forefinger extended, with no movement whatsoever. It might be formed into the shape of a pistol, with the forefinger forward and the thumb extended. The hand might be jabbing as either a question is asked or a statement made, or physically poking someone or something. The act of pointing could include a prop of one kind or another to direct a person's attention, never touching that which is pointed to, or it might be used to tap the material being called to attention, lightly or with a slamming impact.

Suffice it to say that there are at least hundreds of ways to point at something or someone, each conveying its own subliminal and sometimes not so subliminal underlying message, which we will not delve into here. Most important is to be aware that depending on when and how someone points to something or at someone, they are expressing a nonverbal message in combination with their overall body language to which you must be sensitive and receptive. Conversely, extreme care must be exercised when you use this method of illustrating or calling attention in a persuasion situation, as you will also be transmitting a message to your subjects.

If, for example, you wish to call out something specific on a page, use the forefinger to point to it, making sure that the palm of your hand faces the subject, with the other fingers somewhat open. It is never advisable to show the back of your hand or use a clenched fist unless you happen to be dealing with an extremely submissive person and you wish to enforce dominance or intimidation.

If, however, you want to indicate something in general, a good method is to point to it with a completely open hand, fingers extended and palm toward the subject, thus directing his or her attention to the entire page.

The use of props can also be effective. In sales, a pen is most effective and accomplishes two purposes.

First, people subliminally envision a pen in the hand of a salesperson with as much apprehension as they would a gun in the hand of a mugger. The pen is, in their mind, the natural weapon of the salesperson. When he or she takes that pen out, it signals the beginning of the final steps in the process of extracting their money—writing a contract or purchase order—and may cause them to withdraw or resist. Frequent use of the pen in the early stages of the presentation eliminates this fear as the subject becomes accustomed to seeing the pen in the salesperson's hand.

Second, it is a very effective pointer in that it can be used to call attention to something very specific or, used in a sweeping motion, to something in general.

In conjunction with pointing, the pen can also be used to stimulate eye contact. This is accomplished simply by lifting the pen from the page and bringing it very slowly toward your eye as the subject follows the movement.

Also extremely important is the manner in which the pen is held. If you grip it as you would a stick or knife, the image will be one of dominance, aggression, and intimidation. A more neutral and acceptable position is a slight variation of the grip you normally use when actually writing, again holding the palm forward and the fingers loose and comfortable.

Jumping to Body Conclusions

What we verbalize and what we think are often entirely different. When this occurs, we run the risk of contradicting what we're saying by our expression, tone of voice, body language, and gestures, the outward physical signs that represent our true feelings. Unfortunately, many can be easily misinterpreted if diagnosed at the wrong time or under inappropriate circumstances.

For example, what does it mean when someone sits with arms folded and legs crossed? Most people would immediately respond by identifying that posture as defensive and closed-minded. But is this diagnosis always correct? How many times during a day or evening could you find yourself in one or both positions when alone and not involved in conversation with anyone? If someone saw you and claimed that you were defensive and closed-minded, you'd probably say they were crazy, or at least making a mistaken assumption.

The same is true of others. That position might simply mean the person is comfortable in that position. If, however, someone assumes that position immediately after being told something or asked a question, it then signals their nonverbal response and true feelings, giving the professional persuader a distinct advantage.

Legal Use of the Hands

The same is true as it applies to gestures and the positioning of hands. Taken in and of themselves, they indicate nothing. As a response to a statement or question, however, gestures and hand positioning convey very specific meanings. For example:

Hands palms up indicates a desire for more information in a cooperative attitude.

Hands palms down is telling you to slow down. The person is neither agreeing nor disagreeing, but is definitely not with you at this point. It would be wise to ask if they have any questions.

Hands clutching the body is a clear indicator that the subject neither believes nor trusts you or whatever you are telling him. Sometime during the conversation, you slipped and transmitted a contradiction. If at all possible, start from the beginning and be careful!

Hands clutching the chair, table or desk conveys a defensive attitude and attempt to hold back from saying or doing what the subject really desires. Stop and probe for true feelings and emotions, taking special notice of pupil dilation.

Hands on the table, forefinger raised indicates a person who intends to dominate not only you but the conversation. It is going to require moves and countermoves to establish rapport and respect before you'll get anywhere with this individual.

Hands tightly closed in a fist indicates either a naturally aggressive person or one in whom you've created an aggressive response or reflex. Before attempting persuasion of any kind, it will be necessary to calm this person down by allowing them to vent their feelings.

Fingers of one hand pointing to the palm of the other signals that your subject is expecting to receive something in return for their agreement with you. This would be a good time to emphasize specific benefits.

Fingers adjusting glasses might simply mean a bad fit by Lenses-R-Us. Done in direct response to something you're saying, however, the gesture indicates you've hit a particular interest on which your subject wants to see more detail.

Hands clasped behind the head or fingertips steepled in front of the face indicates a desire to establish dominance and superiority, most especially when the head is tilted forward and the eyes focus below the upper eyelids.

Using the hands to groom hair, especially while tilting the head, is a definite sign that you have someone who is really not sure whether or not to agree with you. It's going to take more work.

Using a hand to rub the forehead while simultaneously shading the eyes is an attempt to completely block out what you are saying. He doesn't agree with you, has no intention of listening, and is trying to communicate that you're boring him to tears.

Keeping the hands out of sight, under a table, or in the pockets indicates a person who is aware that their hands communicate feelings and wants to make sure they're not transmitting. They might be deceptive, saying something they really don't mean, or don't want to show their true feelings or interest.

Rubbing the ear is almost always an indicator that you have a person who has told so many lies that even they don't want to hear them anymore.

Scratching the neck is an admission that the subject is telling you something they don't really believe.

Pulling the collar is another admission of deception. This person is lying so much that stress is making it difficult to breathe.

Covering the mouth is a signal that the subject is really trying to hold back what they would like to say, either out of simple courtesy or to avoid a confrontation.

Touching or rubbing areas around the eyes indicates a person who is lying so much they're embarrassed to look at you.

Bodies in Motion

Subliminal messages are also transmitted by other parts of the human anatomy as they move from one position to another in response to a question or statement.

A rigid body moved to the right or left conveys a person's attempt to dodge answering a question or giving agreement.

Tilting the head, especially combined with fixed eye contact and a smile, indicates receptivity and agreement as well as warmth, empathy, and friendship without submissiveness or passivity.

Folding the arms and/or crossing the legs in response to a question or statement are blocking gestures to convey defensiveness, resistance, uncertainty, insecurity, and disagreement. Stubborn enforcement or resistance is compounded when one or both hands are placed on the crossed leg, in essence locking the position. Not insurmountable, these gestures simply tell you to slow down a little and switch to a topic on which the subject can agree.

One leg crossed over the other knee while the foot jabs back and forth tells you that the subject would really prefer to be kicking you but as the next best alternative will settle for thin air.

Lip biting, face picking, scratching, or pulling skin clearly transmits the person's notion that if he can't get away with hurting you, he'll do it to himself.

Touching or playing with the hair, not to be confused with "grooming," is primarily a woman's subliminal transmission of receptivity to a man and what he's saying.

Cradling the chin is generally a man's signal that he's giving serious thought to your proposal, but does not necessarily indicate receptivity or agreement.

Leaning toward you is a subliminal movement indicating not only interest but receptivity, with agreement on the way, especially when accompanied by increased eye contact.

The chin raised to reveal the throat and mouth clamped shut is a universally aggressive, defiant, and challenging posture. This one says you're in for a fight, like it or not, so be prepared to defend yourself.

Mirror, Mirror on the Wall

"Matching and mirroring" is one of the most effective and rapid methods of first establishing and then maintaining rapport with your subject, and accomplishes more than any amount of conversation could ever achieve in the shortest period of time.

When you first begin to use this technique, you may find it uncomfortable and possibly even embarrassing, believing that your subjects are aware of exactly what you're doing. They aren't. In fact, when you're with friends, you mirror each other all the time without being aware of it.

Once you have consciously practiced this technique and discovered how effective it really is, it will become automatic.

Quite simply, if your subject sits with arms folded while in a discussion, leans forward or back, or sits with legs crossed, you do the same. However, contrary to some popular beliefs, matching and mirroring to be effective applies not just to posture or the position of arms and legs, but to the entire person. As emphasized previously, this includes facial expression, use of the eyes, voice intonation, and specific use of words and phrases.

Once you have begun mirroring, you will in a very short period of time actually feel a bond begin to develop, as will your subjects. The difference is that while you are consciously aware of what you are doing, they are not.

A short while later, you will discover another phenomenon. Instead of simply following their lead, you'll be able to initiate moves they will begin to follow. Once this occurs, you will have successfully achieved both a physiological and psychological rapport which you'll discover makes the mental process of communication and persuasion anywhere from 50 percent to upwards of 75 percent more effective than could be achieved without this method.

At some point in the discussion, test their response by changing your seated or standing position. Tilt your head to one side or the other. Change the position of your arms and hands.

For example, let's say you're seated at the table and your subject is sitting in an upright position. Do the same, but after a short period of time, lean slightly forward. If he or she leans back, you know you are invading his or her space and are nowhere near establishing rapport. BACK OFF IMMEDIATELY!

If they remain in the same position, continue to mirror them. If they lean forward, stay in that position, and shortly thereafter, change to another position as a second test. If they follow, YOU HAVE THE LEAD!

Nothing is Insurmountable

Nearly all of the negative attitudes identified by the subliminally negative postures, positions, and gestures described above can usually be countered or changed—first by accurate recognition and interpretation, enabling you to deal with that particular problem; and second by utilizing the techniques of matching and mirroring described in this chapter to ultimately change and lead your subject into a more receptive frame of mind.

The only exception to this is in the area of those postures or gestures which represent defiance, hostility, anger, or challenge. If you mirror these instead of placating your subject, you will hasten a nasty confrontation by subliminally transmitting the same attitude. The only remedy is to acknowledge that at some point during the discussion you were not paying attention to the early warning signals, or that your own subliminal transmissions contradicted what you were attempting to convey verbally, thereby precipitating the current attitude. This would be the time to lay the cards on the table and find out exactly what is bothering the other person before attempting to proceed in what would otherwise be a hopeless situation.

The most important thing to remember is that communication is a two-way process. The ability to recognize and accurately interpret subliminal manifestations of various expressions, postures, and gestures definitely gives you the edge in any persuasion situation. More important, however, is the need to be consciously aware that like your subject, you are also continuously transmitting nonverbal messages. If persuasion is to be effective, it takes a conscious, continuous, and concentrated effort to make sure those messages are in complete harmony with what you are verbalizing.

Saying Farewell, Not Good-bye!

Primary and recency effects are the two areas which take precedence in human recall. In other words, the last impression is just as important as, and in some cases more important than, the first. While the first impression causes a lasting effect throughout the ensuing discussion or conversation, how you part with someone is how they will remember you until and if ever there is another encounter. That parting impression will remain with them longer than any part of the meeting itself. If they feel "rushed and out the door" or if the parting is drawn out to the point that it becomes tedious and boring, that is the impression they will attach to you personally.

The best possible parting is one which is brief but smooth, emphasizing the importance of the very special relationship you feel with the other person. A smile and a firm handshake reinforce those feelings of sincerity, caring, and warmth.

At this point, you have come to recognize and interpret the various signals conveyed both verbally and nonverbally by others, which is a crucial part of the process of persuasion.

The most critical determining factor in your success, however, and by far the most exciting transformation toward consistently effective persuasion, comes with . . .

SUBLIMINAL FITNESS CONDITIONING

7

SUBLIMINAL FITNESS CONDITIONING

Y ou can be whatever you want! You will be as successful as you desire! Visualize yourself succeeding and you will succeed!" are the resounding proclamations of the gurus.

What they don't say is that desire and visualization, while necessary ingredients to achievement, are a mere fraction of the overall formula.

I really wanted to be a pilot. At first, images of breaking the tethers of earthbound problems and soaring in the clear blue sky among billowing snowy-white clouds occupied only my dreams, then progressively became an opiate, addicting me throughout all my waking hours.

I no longer merely *wanted* to be a pilot. I *had* to become a pilot, to fly or eventually become nothing more than a vegetable of thoughts, dreams, and hopes, staring at the sky as a prisoner might gaze through the window bars of his cell at freedom, only inches away yet always just out of reach.

Once my desire was strong enough and I could clearly visualize being a pilot, I drove to the nearest airport, hopped into a plane, and within minutes was airborne at five thousand feet, enthralled in the ecstasy of spins, barrel rolls, and hammerhead aerobatics.

If you believe that, you're buying exactly what the gurus are selling. In flying, it will get you killed. In a career, it will lead you to financial ruin and failure because it only gives you an infinitesimal part of what it takes to succeed.

"That's not true," you might say. "They tell us exactly what to do. Positive thinking, set your goals, and visualize success with en-THU-siasm!"

Right! And all the rest of the myths, because it's easy to tell anyone what they *can* do.

How to do it is another matter entirely!

People said, "Craig, you can be a pilot. It'll be easy for someone like you," and I immediately agreed with them, praising their intelligence, wisdom, incredible judgment of character, and ability to recognize my true potential and talents. Not once did I consider that none of them had ever actually flown a plane!

When a pilot friend of mine asked if I realized exactly what I was getting into—the amount of time studying; the hours with an instructor doing what would quickly become repetitive, mundane, and boring procedures; the work it would take; and the money I'd spend before even coming close to getting licensed, much less realizing my dream—I began to wonder just how much of a friend he really was.

In fact, it wasn't until after I began flight school that I came to value him as a true friend who was willing to tell it to me exactly as it was rather than merely boosting my ego.

I realized two things. First, people are always quick to tell someone else how easy it is to do something, especially when they haven't done it themselves. And second, the majority of people don't really want to hear how difficult something might be once they've made the decision to do it. They want to hear how effortless, quick, and inexpensive it is. They want to learn the "secrets" to achieving something the easy way.

That's why, for example, billions of dollars are spent in this country on diet pills, drinks, and programs which require "little or no exercise." When one doesn't work, people simply go on to the next, and the next, and the next, with no lasting results, all the while deluding themselves into thinking that somewhere there's this magic, effortless solution, all the while avoiding the real answer because they don't want to confront it.

Those programs are a perfect testimonial to the effective results of subliminal power persuasion. The marketers realize their prospects' motivators (ego, envy, pride, vanity, survival), recognize the stimulator (weight loss), and simply tell them what they want to hear (easy, quick, effortless, inexpensive, no exercising). Bingo! Persuasion accomplished!

That's not what we're doing here. As a matter of fact, the purpose of this book is neither to motivate you with how easy persuasion can be nor tell you how to be a one-minute success story, because neither is possible.

True motivation does not come from an outside source. It's like integrity, character, drive, ambition, and tenacity. If you don't already have it, or have not made the decision to begin developing it, you won't find it in any book or seminar.

Neither is the purpose of this book to persuade you, but instead to tell you like it really is. Very much like the true friend who told me what was involved in learning to fly, to realize my dream of soaring among the clouds, reaching heights I'd never before imagined, I'm telling you that to be effective at persuasion takes work, like anything else, to achieve consistent, positive results. It takes belief. It takes commitment. But even before that, it takes . . .

Subliminal Fitness Conditioning

Once a pilot has acquired all the knowledge and skills necessary to fly a plane, but prior to boarding an aircraft, he or she has to take some preliminary steps to prevent any possibility of mistakes or errors, just one of which could have disastrous results in a procedure in which there are few second chances.

First, the weather is checked and a flight plan filed that designates the point of departure, the final destination, and the anticipated flight route, any of which may be modified based upon unforeseen circumstances. Next comes the "walk-around" inspection of the outside of the aircraft to make sure it's in good shape and ready for flight. Inside the cockpit, there's the preflight checklist to make sure everything is operating properly and that the correct program is entered.

Regardless of the number of hours logged, or how well they know the procedures, every qualified, experienced pilot goes through this checklist each and every time before starting the engines, confident that having accomplished the preliminaries, the only surprises will be those encountered in flight, which are then handled as they arise.

Unlike flying an airplane, the process of persuasion does give you second chances, but it still requires exactly that same amount of care, diligence, and discipline to be effective. Throughout this book, you have acquired the knowledge, skills, and techniques for consistent, successful persuasion. You know the mechanics of flying this plane, and you'll continue to learn and improve your skills with the experience of each and every flight. But before you even step into the cockpit, what about the aircraft, the equipment, and its programming? What about the checklist?

What about you?

All the knowledge, techniques, and skills aren't worth a cent if you don't have the proper vehicle, and in the persuasion process, **you are that vehicle.**

Way back in this book we talked about recognizing the "programming" of our subjects and arriving at an intimate understanding of them, their drives and motivators. But before you can begin to come to an intimate understanding and appreciation of others, you must first have an even more intimate understanding of yourself. Because unless your self-confidence, skill, poise, and professionalism come from within, you cannot possibly project those things to others.

Each and every one of us has flaws to overcome in order to achieve what we want from life. As we've already seen, most of them were programmed very early in our development by the subconscious mind, based upon circumstances or inadequate information. When allowed to gain a foothold, those limiting programs then formed the basis upon which we act, think, and reason the rest of our lives.

Looking at some of these limiting programs, you might wonder how a reasoning, logical person could possibly base their actions upon them. If you look closely, however, you might be surprised to see one or more of them present in someone you know . . . someone you see every day . . . in the mirror!

Conscious Reprogramming

There Are Formulas for Success as Well as Failure

If a chemist mixes specific amounts of three solutions and the result is an explosion, has he failed? If the explosion was what he wanted to achieve, it was a success. If the explosion was not what he expected, it was simply an unforeseen result. Mixing those exact solutions a second time and expecting different results, however, would not be a mistake or an unforeseen result. At that point it would be a failure, and a needless one at that.

The same is true in life, relationships, and business. By experience, we learn formulas for success and formulas for failure, but all too often don't recognize them as such.

Doing anything on a repetitive basis and experiencing a specific result assures you that the same exact process will always yield the same exact result.

People who succeed recognize this concept and continue to succeed. Those who refuse to recognize it continue to fail.

If you opened five businesses and each of them failed, how many more would you open before finally taking a job as an employee and giving up the dream of owning your own company? If every time you introduced yourself to someone you felt was extremely attractive and they abruptly ended the conversation by looking at you as if you had three eyes and then turned and walked away, how many times would you approach someone like that until you finally settled for less? If you just began your career in sales and after the first twenty-five calls had not made a sale, how many more would you make before coming to the conclusion that selling is just not in the cards for you as a career?

Once more? Twice? Maybe three times?

People stop trying to accomplish something only when they decide it's really not worth the effort, they are afraid of repeated failure, and/or because they refuse to change their approach to accomplish successful results. If Thomas Edison looked at things that way after five hundred designs which did not work, he would never have tried nearly five hundred more until he came up with what we know today as a light bulb! If the Wright brothers looked at things that way, they would never have designed an airplane which got off the ground.

Yet each succeeded because they refused to believe that failure in the past automatically results in failure in the future, and they were determined to continue to use different procedures to achieve the desired success. They believed that instead of failing, each and every attempt brought them closer to *what would work* by showing them *what did not work* and forcing them to change their approach.

You Cannot Fail!

If you knew that starting today, you couldn't possibly fail at any-thing you decided to do, what could you do? The obvious an-swer is anything you want! Take your pick! So what's stopping you?

The fact of the matter is that if you desire anything enough to make a commitment to its accomplishment, take the nec-essary action to achieve it, avoid duplicating patterns you know from experience will not work, and adjust your plan when you see it is not bringing about the desired result, you cannot fail and in fact will eventually succeed!

Each and every action will have a positive result, showing you the way to accomplish your objective or illustrating yet an-other method which will not work.

The "If Only" and "What If" Traps

As stated in a previous chapter, different people have different subliminal motivators in varying degrees. Everyone, however, is dominated to the extreme by two of them: attraction to plea-sure and aversion to pain or discomfort.

While the attraction to pleasure and subsequent satisfaction of other motivators or combination of motivators play a major role, the subliminal will *always* place a higher priority on the most powerful and dominant motivator, aversion to pain, loss, and rejection. In doing so, it will provide a limitless number of excuses not to do something in which there is the slightest risk.

These excuses are usually based upon deficiencies (if onlys) and/or fear of the unknown (what ifs) to avoid the possibility of failure. "If only I had the money. If only I had a college education. If only I were older. If only I were younger. If only I had the contacts. If only I were thin. If only I were more well built. If only I were more attractive."

Fulfilling the primary purpose of protecting its subject, the subliminal will always focus on the negatives of a situation.

"I would really like to approach that person, but what if he completely rejects me? I'd be worse off than I am right now because of yet another rejection."

"I want in the worst way to start my own business, to do what I really enjoy doing, and to chart the course of my own destiny, but what if I put everything I own into it and it goes down the tubes? I'll be right back where I am now, working for someone else but without any savings in the bank."

"I know I'm overweight and should do something about my eating habits, but what if I fail? I'll still be fat and overweight with yet another failure in my past, feeling worse than I do right now."

The human mind is the most perfect computer in the world, operating an entire chemical plant completely on its own, coordinating both physical and mental functions, each of which has its own purpose, without your conscious attention. Accepting that, it becomes easy to see why this particular motivator is built into all of us. It is, in fact, a conditioned reflex which negatively responds to any action, idea, circumstance, or situation with which it is not familiar. Automatically and instantaneously balancing and in some cases completely offsetting the attraction to pleasure motivator, it's the one that makes you stop and consciously think a second time, "Do I really want it that badly?" and for a very good reason.

In the example of the boy driven by the ego motivator to walk the length of a plank five hundred feet off the ground to impress his friends, aversion to pain makes him stop and think, "But what if I fall?" If the survival motivator has priority, it will dominate. If the ego is stronger, he'll proceed. Either way, the subliminal has done its job. That's the positive side.

Unfortunately, this function can also be the most limiting of the subliminal, which has a built-in **resistance to change**. By prompting fear of the unknown, it inhibits people from progressing, from taking steps which may involve risk but also opportunity.

Creating conditioning by association, the subliminal conveys instantaneous images to the conscious mind to stop an action or response by stimulating negative thoughts of what "might" happen.

The salesperson who is conditioned to earning X amount, for example, suddenly thinks about doing something different, more creative than he has ever done, to increase sales. The subliminal responds by manufacturing thoughts of losing not only new accounts but those already established.

Turning the Subliminal Inside-Out

Colonel Sanders did not decide to start his famous chain until he received his first social security check and became determined to do something better with his life.

And he is far from alone . . . like the woman I know who, in her late forties, decided to start college and get her degree. Family and friends all tried to discourage her. "My gosh, Beth. Do you realize that by the time you graduate, you'll be in your fifties?" Her response was, "And if I don't, years from now I'll *still* be in my fifties and *still* without my college degree. That's why I'm going to do it!"

The first step to overriding the negative results of the subliminal aversion to pain motivator is to make the mental commitment to change. Not that I should, could, or might, but that I WILL!

The next step is to reprogram the subliminal computer and conditioned response by turning the aversion to pain motivator against itself by using the "what if" response. Instead of concentrating on the pain of taking the action, create and visualize a detailed negative picture of the results of *not* taking the action to the point that you actually see yourself in that situation, becoming more and more uncomfortable.

"What if I *don't* approach that person or, for that matter, anyone who really appeals to me? In that case I can count on spending the rest of my life either alone or with someone I'm really not attracted to, becoming more and more miserable over the years!"

"What if I *don't* take that shot at opening the business I dream about? I'll have to spend the rest of my life working in a job I hate with no opportunity of advancement. As my savings dwindle and I grow older, with increasing financial difficulties, I'll wonder for the rest of my life what would have happened if I'd only taken that step!"

"What if I *don't* get my eating under control? I'll end up getting heavier and heavier, my self-image will deteriorate with every pound, people will look at me pityingly, and it's only a matter of time before health problems end my life prematurely."

Actually *see* yourself five years from now, the situation five times worse than it is today. Visualize the way you'd look to yourself and other people. Feel the emotional and physical pain of being in a worse situation, even more hopeless than before!

Now put yourself ten years in the future. Feel the loneliness, the despair, the failure, knowing that long ago it could have been avoided simply by taking the necessary steps to change. But now it just keeps getting worse, all the negatives compounding as you see yourself more frustrated, disappointed, and completely unhappy with your life. Get a good, clear picture and hold it in front of your mind's eye. Get upset! Get mad! Feel the frustration and hopelessness of no possible solution! No way out! Trapped in a life of misery!

Now form a new picture. See yourself as you are now, not yet as you want to be in that relationship, business of your own, physical condition, or circumstance specific to you, but at least relieved to know that the visualizations you just created are not reality . . . not yet, that is!

Now change the channel. See yourself improving a little at a time, actually doing the things you know are necessary to change your life, improving year after year, actually doing all the things you want to in your life, feeling the comfort, joy, and pride of accomplishment as you take the necessary steps to achievement.

Performing this exercise on a purposeful, consistent basis, really experiencing the emotions, seeing and feeling yourself physically in a setting you desire, will, with repetition, automatically reprogram your subliminal. By changing your conditioning and subsequent associations, a new pattern takes hold and you will quickly discover yourself thinking more positively about yourself without concentrating on the exercise. In a very short period of time, the uncomfortable visualizations will diminish, replaced by longer periods of seeing yourself as you desire.

As this process continues, your subliminal, having accepted the new program, methodically begins to bring those visualizations to reality as you find yourself "unconsciously" acting and making decisions along a completely different pattern from that you would have previously followed.

> *"Great spirits have always encountered violent opposition from mediocre minds!"*   —ALBERT EINSTEIN

There is no way of knowing just how far we might have progressed in industry, technology, health care, or simply everyday comfort if the combination of the words "That's a really stupid idea!" had never been formed.

Fear of rejection and need for approval are another part of the aversion to pain and attraction to pleasure motivators, both working in exactly the same way to impede progress, new ideas, forward thinking, and improved lifestyles. Millions walk through life making decisions and taking actions based solely upon what other people might think of them, people who, in turn, are basing their lives on the opinions of yet others.

"Average" People Are Only Average Because There Are So Many of Them

If you base your ideas and actions on the way other people think or, worse yet, on what they will think of you, you'll never get farther ahead than they are.

All revolutionary ideas began with a concept ridiculed by "average" people with "average" mentalities. The very thought that the horse and buggy would be replaced by some mechanical contraption on four wheels was a joke. The idea that people would ever think of traveling from one city to another in one of those flying machines was ludicrous.

Some years ago, executives at IBM laughed at the idea of computers being designed and marketed to the general public for personal use, and it wasn't that long ago that General Motors thought it was hilarious to think that Americans would ever consider purchasing smaller automobiles, especially from Japan! And the notion that people would ever pump their own gas? Everyone knew you had to give free sets of glassware just to get them to come into a station!

Yes, those were really stupid ideas. So said not only "average" people, but also The Experts.

The best ideas and greatest innovations in the world are buried in the graveyard because someone said they sounded like stupid ideas and someone else took his word for it.

Constantly looking for approval is a primary symptom of insecurity. It confirms that you value another's opinion more than your own, and as long as you continue to do that, you will never gain the self-confidence to succeed, whatever your personal definition of success. As shown in "Exploding the Myths," even when you do succeed, people prefer to criticize rather than approve. "He (or she) was lucky, he got the breaks, he had an unfair advantage" will be the "average" comments from "average" people who hate the thought of anyone rising above their ranks.

The only person whose approval you absolutely require is

the one with whom you spend the most time, twenty-four hours each and every day of your life.

I Really Don't Deserve This

Guilt, either actual or imagined, is one of the most frequent, insidious, and limiting of all subliminal programming, manifesting itself in so many ways that entire books have been written to describe and analyze them. All, however, have one common ingredient: self-sabotage.

People laboring under this programming are seldom consciously aware of it. In the few instances when they are, they attempt to deny it because it brings back memories of the action which precipitated the original guilt. These are people whose lives, when things seem to be going their way, always take a turn for the worse and they lose not only the ground they've gained, but more. What they don't realize is that when life took a turn for the worse, they're usually the ones who took that turn.

In relationships beginning to reach a fruitful and productive level, they'll suddenly find a reason to move away, initiate arguments which have no validity, drift apart, or lose interest in the other person for no apparent or sound reason. Finding themselves in a position of sudden prosperity as the result of productivity on a job or other source, they'll squander money uncontrollably, realizing they are doing it on things which would not previously have entered their mind, but never understanding why and being completely unable to stop.

Most often they attribute the reason directly to themselves. "Why did I do that to myself? How could I have been so stupid as to say that? What could I possibly have been thinking? Why did I move in that direction?" are typical questions.

The primary reason, the one they don't recognize or most often don't want to acknowledge, is guilt. It originates in the notion that they really don't deserve good things happening in their present or future due to some real or imagined blame they accept and harbor from the past.

Guilt, or what some call "conscience," especially in the subliminal, demands its due. Unfortunately, both the guilt and the punishment people inflict upon themselves is limitless, demanding many times the price for even the smallest transgression until reprogramming occurs.

We are all products of our decisions up to and including this very moment. Some of those decisions were good and we benefited from them. Others were damaging, for which we were accountable and paid the price.

Good or bad, those decisions are in the past. They were made under emotions and circumstances we can't relive and may in fact have been totally correct at the time. But whether the decisions were right or wrong, the results cannot be undone or changed. Yet each and every one provided a formula which we have the choice to either repeat or avoid.

To go through life carrying guilt from the past is to live in the past with no hope of improvement or growth for the future. That is a punishment no one deserves.

Victims of Circumstance

Although some people like to attribute their position in life to circumstances, little could be farther from the truth. Since we are all the product of our decisions up to this very moment, we will also be the product of decisions we make in the future. The circumstances in which we live are the results of our past decisions, and those which befall us are usually also a result of decisions for which only we can take responsibility.

Granted, things will happen which are often out of our control and not a direct result of a decision on our part. Yet in the response to each, we have choices and alternatives available to determine not where we have been, but instead where we are going.

By making those decisions, and then taking responsibility for them, we can then take both credit for and action toward our destiny.

He Just Ruined My Whole Day!

You can have a perfectly good day with things going exactly the way you want when suddenly someone says or does something to irritate you. A husband and wife get into an argument before they leave for work. An employee gets called on the carpet by a supervisor. From that point on, some people become so flustered they can't properly perform. Whose fault is that? The other person's, naturally.

As a matter of fact, no one and nothing can ruin your day or your mood but you! You are the person who dictates your mood, your frame of reference, and then puts yourself into it. Do you want to be angry, sad, depressed, happy, enthusiastic? Go ahead and do it, but don't blame or credit anyone else for it because you are the one in total control of your emotions.

If not, you can be.

In "nonverbal subliminal persuasion" you learned how people communicate with their eyes, body, gestures, positions, and expressions even more than with the spoken word and in fact more truthfully. What we often tend to forget is that what's true of others is also true of ourselves.

Our physical profile is a response to our true feelings and emotions. You get mad, you look mad. You feel disappointment, you look disappointed. You get depressed, you look depressed. It's simply a conditioned response whereby any emotion you feel is reflected in your physiology, and to deny that part of our life would be unrealistic and contrary to human nature. Allowing it to continue, however, is completely up to you and totally within your control.

People allow a certain mood to continue for a long period of time for only one reason. Consciously or subconsciously they want everyone to know just how they feel, so they communicate it for agreement, acceptance, approval, or any number of the prime motivators and satisfiers which dominate their psyche.

How long, for example, would a person who is angry continue to rant, rave, stomp, and shout if nobody was around to see their anger? Granted, the initial response to something will be there but for it to continue over the course of time when that person is alone would indicate the need for some serious professional help, a straitjacket, or a rubber room.

What few realize and want to believe is that while they go out of their way to make their feelings known to others, those people might initially respond but after a short time don't really care! So why bother?

If someone experiences the loss of a person to whom they

are very close and communicate their feelings to you, you'll probably express sympathy. But if this continues over a period of time it will become extremely boring and tiresome to the point that you'll begin to avoid that person as much as possible. What most people don't want to believe is that others react to them in exactly the same way.

The gurus say that you simply have to get yourself "pumped up" to get out of a certain frame of mind. But how do you do that? You can try to think of other things, but the old tapes continue in playback mode.

For the answer, look to women.

Most women I know, when things aren't going their way, go shopping for new clothes! The reason is not in the actual buying, but rather in what the shopping entails. If a woman enjoys shopping, and I don't know many who do not, she begins looking forward to the activity. She goes to the mall or the avenue among other people and starts looking at new clothes, trying things on, really enjoying the experience, standing straight in front of a mirror and seeing herself in a different outfit, a different style, a different light, a different mood, and yes, even as a different woman.

Any parent will tell you that one of the quickest ways to stop a child from being sad or crying is to make him or her laugh with funny faces or even tickling. You and I are no different from that child.

If you really want to become and stay depressed, think depressing thoughts, get yourself slumped over, walk with an aimless shuffle and a frown on your face. Carry the cross on your back and tell everyone how bad things are and soon you'll find people avoiding you, which will then compound your misery.

On the other hand, could you really continue to be depressed or angry for any length of time if you focus on the positive parts of your life, stand tall and straight, a big smile on your face, a brisk and confident stride in your step? It would be physically and emotionally impossible. You, after all, are completely in control of your physiology and therefore your mood, focus, and attitude.

"I Can't Stand the Way (S)He Treats Me!"

One of the most widely publicized issues today is sexual harassment. In reality, it is simply another form of intimidation and there are an endless number of jerks of both sexes who use this technique to compensate for their own inferiority, ineptitude, incompetence, and miserable self-image.

Like street-corner bullies, they enjoy preying upon people who send out either or both verbal and nonverbal signals of weakness, passivity, inability to defend themselves, or a willingness and in some cases a proclivity to be abused, insulted, and mistreated.

And that is the fault of the victim.

Myth #5 emphasizes that you cannot be effective if you either believe or project the belief that you are subservient to anyone.

RESPECT YOURSELF! If you don't, no one else will!

There is no reason in the world why you should put up with or be exposed to annoying, obnoxious behavior from anyone! Only by making it very evident that you will not tolerate or expose yourself to it will it cease.

Your Focus = YOUR RESULTS

The subliminal is our lifelong companion . . . and slave. It does whatever we tell it.

Did you ever have a problem of one kind or another nagging at you to the point that the more you thought about trying to come up with an answer, the more complicated it became? Then one night you went to bed, fell asleep wondering about possible solutions, and woke up the next morning with the answer so crystal clear that you wondered why you'd never thought of it before?

Most people consciously focus on problems, constantly reinforcing them. By focusing on arriving at solutions, however, you assign the task to your subliminal, which, in keeping with its responsibility to you, does exactly as it is told.

This function is not, however, limited to problem solving. Since the subliminal cannot distinguish between fantasy and reality, it always works on the basis of our focus. As we focus on ourselves, that's what we become. When the child, constantly reminded of being worthless and stupid, begins to focus on him- or herself that way, in the mind's eye, that focus becomes reality.

The aversion to pain motivator works the same way. It keeps individuals focusing on themselves exactly as they are without risking the possible unknown dangers of attempting to change or improve.

If you want to be unhappy, focus on all the unhappy events of your life. In fact, most people can always find something negative to focus on because those are the easiest for the "average" person. The hypochondriac who spends the majority of his waking hours studying and worrying about diseases and their symptoms can actually produce the physical symptoms and the disease itself. People who constantly worry about financial difficulties continue to have a never-ending supply of them. People who are extremely jealous and insecure, always worrying about the possibility of their spouses having an extramarital affair, often unconsciously do things to drive them to exactly that which they fear and suspect most. Those who constantly worry about losing their jobs are usually the first to go. The salesperson who worries and wonders, "Why do I keep losing sales? . . . keep losing sales . . . keep losing sales . . . keep losing sales!"

What's the message to the subliminal?

Instead of focusing on solutions, these people focus on problems, thereby compounding them, putting them into their subliminal, and in effect saying, "Here, keep working on this." And it does, creating anxiety, which further complicates the problem, setting up a self-fulfilling prophecy. People react by trying harder. The result: the harder you try, the behinder you get!

The same method, used differently, can be just as effective on the positive side.

Let's assume that you want to be more successful. The first step is determining the definition of success as it applies to you. If it's a bigger house, a larger bank account, or a yacht in the harbor, get a vivid picture of those things in your mind.

Next, how would you look if you were more successful? Would you be dressed differently? How would people react to you at business and social functions? See it in your mind in detail. Listen to the conversations. See yourself giving a presentation to others and listen to them applaud your innovative ideas and concepts.

The person who wants to increase sales begins to focus on, "How do I make more sales and enjoy my job more while doing it better?" all the while seeing him- or herself closing one sale after another. "Make more sales . . . do it better . . . enjoy it more!" becomes the message to the subliminal. The person thinks as often of these pictures as they previously did about financial problems and poverty.

But these are just examples. Yours might be completely different. Your goal might be better and more loving relationships. It might be having the ability to make a more productive contribution to a cause. Whatever it is, by picturing it precisely in your mind, concentrating on doing it better and more efficiently, seeking out ways to improve, and then being willing to take the necessary actions, you change your focus and, automatically, your reality.

What the Mind Expects Tends to Be Realized

Hypnosis is a process of expectation and believability, first by the conscious and then by the subconscious or subliminal mind. The hypnotist looks directly into the subject's eyes and in a very matter-of-fact and confident voice tells them exactly what to expect, makes it believable, and repeats it for reinforcement. "When I snap my fingers, you will drift into a very deep, very pleasant state. Each and every time I snap my fingers after that you will go one step deeper, and deeper, and deeper."

If at this point the subject breaks into hysterical laughter, the professional hypnotist realizes it's time to quit right then and there. However, if the subject's eyes begin to blink, tear, or lower, it indicates a prime candidate who truly believes and expects what has been described, consciously as well as subconsciously. At that point belief becomes reality. Under hypnosis people have even undergone surgery without experiencing pain and recuperated in 50 percent less time than those who had anesthetics.

"What the mind expects tends to be realized" has been demonstrated countless times: the Olympic weightlifter who pressed 500 pounds only because he thought he was pressing the 498 pounds he had already done several times previously; the 4-minute mile, which was considered an unbreakable record until Roger Bannister accomplished it, quickly followed by 32 others in the very next month.

Although the above are dramatic illustrations, we program and then reinforce our belief system every day in the smallest, most subtle ways. The golfer, for example, who digs around in his bag for a cut or damaged ball to play when confronted by a water hazard is actually reinforcing the belief that he is bound and determined to hit the pond, then wonders why he always does just that.

Fortunately, what can be programmed can just as easily be deprogrammed, as you will see later in the chapter.

If Not Me, Who? If Not Now, When?

Procrastination is another self-limiting program caused by one or more motivators, most often aversion to pain or discomfort (doing it) or attraction to pleasure (doing something else you enjoy).

When procrastination is merely a sporadic response to particularly annoying tasks, the simple solution is to reverse the motivator against itself.

"What will happen if I don't do it now? I'll push it forward until tomorrow and the next day and the next until finally I'll have no choice and be forced into the situation anyway, but with less time to get it done and no opportunity to deal with any unforeseen circumstances should they arise."

Visualize the discomfort of having the task hanging over your head, day after day, always aware of it being there regardless of how much or how often you attempt to put it aside, until it's finally forced upon you. Now visualize the freedom of finally having it completed and the ability to get on with more pleasant activities with a clear mind, able to fully enjoy them.

Sporadic procrastination is common with everyone. Habitual procrastination, however, reflects a much deeper subliminal programming difficulty.

"If I really got on the stick and took advantage of this situation, I might be more successful than I really deserve to be, or than I should be. The easy solution is simply to put it off until the opportunity passes."

Reversing procrastination will be of little or no help in this case since the root of the problem is not procrastination, but rather a program of self-imposed guilt or a poor self-image. Here, the guilt or limitation must be turned against itself to initiate reprogramming of the person's focus.

Performed on a repetitive basis, conscious reprogramming is effective because it eventually enters the subconscious or subliminal to effect the necessary changes, depending on how often it's performed and the depth of the negative programming.

While the methods described above are extremely effective in changing behavior, they are performed on a conscious basis, relying on repetition to eventually permeate the subliminal, wherein lies the source of the problem. Their effect and the time involved to reprogram the subliminal is altered by distraction, lack of ability to concentrate in certain circumstances or under adverse conditions, and the depth of the negative programming. Eventually, however, constant repetition will win out and the methods do and will work.

Subliminal Reprogramming

Subliminal reprogramming, when used alone or especially in conjunction with conscious reprogramming, goes directly to the subconscious, involves no concentration whatsoever, and often results in even faster results.

Before describing what works so effectively, however, it's important to first describe what doesn't work at all.

Why "Subliminal" Audio Tapes Don't Work

"Want to change your life? Be more dynamic, ambitious, imaginative, creative, and enthusiastic? Want to quit smoking, drinking, completely lose your appetite for fattening foods, and find a new slim, trim body in that mirror?

"Too much work, you say? Not at all. All you have to do is sit back, relax, put on the headphones, and listen to the soothing sound of ocean waves. The reason this works is because literally thousands of 'subliminally' imbedded messages you can't hear under any circumstances will be reprogramming your subconscious to get rid of all those nasty habits. In fact, other than sending us three hundred ninety-five dollars for the complete set, you won't have to make any effort at all."

Not too many years ago, "subliminal" audio tapes were the rage for everything from weight reduction to behavior modification to improved learning skills. People were walking around with Walkmans and headsets, listening to everything from the sound of ocean waves to thunderstorms, all to change their lives.

> According to Gordon Deckert, a Davis Ross Boyd Professor of Psychiatry and Behavioral Sciences at the University of Oklahoma Health Sciences Center, the selling of subliminal (audio) tapes is nothing other than a new sort of con game. . . . "There's a child in all of us that would like to believe in magic, so there is what is called a placebo effect with the use of these tapes. A placebo only seems to work. There's certainly no magic solution, nor is there any evidence I know of that these tapes used to change thinking patterns do any better than other actions. They kind of become substitutes for really taking a look at what's going on. Most people would be just as well off setting fire to their money."
> USA Today, September, 1989

Although at one time considered a fifty-million-dollar-a-year business, so-called subliminal tapes used in studies conducted by laboratories and universities failed to produce the results their advertisers claimed in areas of confidence, creativity, ambition, elimination of bad habits, and even weight loss. In fact, the majority of tests, using highly technical and sensitive equipment, determined that few, if any, contained subliminal messages of any kind.

Even when so-called subliminal messages *are* imbedded in audio tapes, they are absolutely impossible to identify by either the conscious or subconscious. In effect, they might as well not be there at all.

This is similar in effect to the sound of a dog whistle. While the sound is easily audible to a dog's ears, it is at a frequency inaudible to the human ear and therefore cannot be distinguished, consciously or subconsciously.

Having put that issue to rest, let's now look at subliminal reprogramming which does work!

You Can't Skip the Commercial

If you're like millions of Americans, the TV commercial signals when it's time to go to the kitchen for a snack. If you're listening to the radio in the car on the way to work, you just ignore it for twenty seconds or so if you're too lazy to change the station.

So why do companies pay millions of dollars for radio and TV commercials? Because they know that even if you leave the room, you'll still hear the commercial. If you change the channel to another station, you'll probably encounter yet another commercial running at the same time. One way or another, they'll eventually get you to buy their product because . . .

Commercials Do Work!

How else would you know what product "spells relief"? What comes to mind when you hear "the uncola," the one that gives you "the right thing, baby, uh-huh!", the drink they call "the king of beers," or the one which is "less filling, tastes great!"

As you consciously direct your attention elsewhere, your subconscious or subliminal mind is wide open and receptive to the very commercial you think you're ignoring.

In recent years this has even been documented in surgical rooms. Anesthetized patients later recalled, under hypnosis, actual word-for-word conversations which took place between surgeons and attendants during operations; those statements came directly from the subconscious or subliminal.

This is exactly what makes the commercial so powerful, selling you both consciously and subliminally on the use of hundreds of products every single day—what they can do for you, the kind of person you can be, and the kind of people you will attract when you use them. The more you are exposed to them, and the less you are consciously aware of them, the more powerful their effect.

This provides another yet little-known tool to assist in changing your focus to reprogram the subliminal.

If every time you turned on the radio you heard a commercial about a particular person who is successful, energetic, determined, and accomplished, who always makes the correct decisions and contributes to the happiness and well-being of others, you would probably be very impressed with that person. Eventually, however, you would begin to tune the commercial out, concentrating on other things. Nevertheless, the message would continue imbedding itself in your subliminal and the more you consciously ignored it, the deeper and more effective it would be implanted.

What do you suppose the effect would be if that person were you!

Your Own Commercial

Assume you work for an advertising agency and your assignment is to write a publicity commercial for someone. You'd want to know what this person does, their qualities, what makes them most attractive and appealing, what makes them stand out above everyone. That's exactly how to write your own commercial, but instead of including only the qualities you now possess, combine them with those you want to have in the future as if they actually existed in the present.

Since everyone has different motivators, programming, and aspirations, there is no single commercial which applies universally. The following, therefore, is merely an example or foundation upon which to base your own.

> (Your name) is one of the most dynamic, ambitious, attractive, confident, and successful (men/women) in (city/state/the nation) today.
> Earning more than (your desired income) a year, (your name)'s success is a reality, having already earned the reputation as one of the top (your profession) in the business at this time, at this moment.
> Most who know (him/her) attribute (your name)'s success to (his/her) dynamic outlook on every situation, (his/her) complete and total confidence, (his/her) ambitious drive to seek opportunities in every situation, and (his/her) uncanny

ability and determination to take whatever steps are necessary, immediately and without procrastination, to turn those opportunities into reality.

(Your name) feels good about (him/her)self, having a high degree of self-esteem and self-worth, realizing the good (he/she) accomplishes not only for (him/her)self but for others. In (his/her) discussions, (your name) demonstrates an honest concern for people, and projects intelligence, power, and confidence in (his/her) ability and willingness to assist them.

When you meet (your name), you see before you a healthy, attractive (man/woman) who immediately impresses you with (his/her) determination, professionalism, ability, and positive, dynamic attitude. (He/she) is the type of person who is successful in everything (he/she) undertakes, drawing wealth, achievement, and other successful, attractive people to (his/her)self like a magnet attracts steel, continually using a combination of creativity, intelligence, imagination, common sense, confidence, and determination in everything (he/she) does. Everyone is immediately impressed with (his/her) successful, friendly good nature, which literally radiates energy and vitality.

(He/she) has the respect of those around (him/her) and everything (he/she) could ever want, living a happy, successful life full of achievement, satisfaction, and happiness, and spreading that happiness to all who come in contact with (him/her).

(He/she) is self-confident and more fortunate than (he/she) has ever been in (his/her) whole life, knowing that whatever (he/she) decides to do automatically results in success, success even beyond and even faster than (he/she) could possibly imagine. And (he/she) realizes this, can see it, can feel it. (He/she) feels good about the image (he/she) presents to people and the conversations (he/she) hears them having about (him/her).

In (his/her) relationships, (your name) automatically attracts those (he/she) desires and is completely secure, providing more than would be expected of anyone and receiving the same in turn.

(He/she) is more creative than (he/she) ever before felt possible. In fact, (his/her) mind is a veritable warehouse of new and exciting ideas and whenever (he/she) desires, (he/she) simply relaxes, closes (his/her) eyes, and those ideas spring forth, bringing with them new thoughts, new plans, and a sense of accomplishment (he/she) never before imagined possible.

(Your name) is the type of person to whom solutions to problems come automatically, quickly, easily, and logically. (He/she) is one of those successful (men/women) who views challenges with a cheerful, ambitious enthusiasm and excitement, knowing that everything (he/she) attempts will ultimately result in success.

(He/she) is healthy, vibrant, full of energy, and attractive, with a metabolism and nervous system which instantly reacts to and immediately overcomes any illness or disease which may attack (him/her). (Your name) enjoys and looks forward to regular exercise and activity, relieving any stress which may build from time to time, and desires only the foods which are healthy and nutritious, increasing (his/her) vitality, energy, and unending stamina. (He/she) easily rids (him/her)self of bad habits and unwanted desires and on a daily basis is feeling more healthy and happy than ever before.

(His/her) life is now an exciting challenge which (he/she) is truly capable of meeting successfully. Every day is a pleasure, bringing something different, something new, something exciting, new events, new people, new ideas.

Anything which would have been considered a problem in the past now merely means a new and exciting opportunity because (he/she) realizes that problems and adversities are really nothing more than opportunities in disguise.

(His/her) life is more and more rewarding because (he/she) makes it so every day and in everything (he/she) does. Because now, everything (he/she) does and says is positive and confident—positive for (his/her) own life as well as the lives of others who come in contact with (him/her), confident because (he/she) has been and is now successful. (He/she) knows that all the good things which happen to (him/her) result from (his/her) magnetic attitude, which attracts only good things and all (he/she) desires.

Now (he/she) has a definite purpose, a definite goal of becoming an even better (profession) than (he/she) already is, a goal toward which (he/she) is moving swiftly, closer every day, already feeling and seeing its accomplishment.

When (he/she) has a task before (him/her), (your name) immediately accomplishes it with ability, determination, and power, looking forward to the challenge and ultimate rewards of which (he/she) is confident.

Everything (your name) does results in success, wealth, and happiness beyond (his/her) dreams, flowing to (him/her) like a river to the sea.

Over and above all, (your name)'s security lies within (him/her)self and (his/her) own confidence in (his/her) abilities and talent. (Your name) is completely happy with (his/her) life as it is now, as it improves day after day, and with (his/her) prospects for the future.

(Your name) is truly successful.

Again, this is merely a format to follow in creating a commercial. Personalize it. Insert your own thoughts, aspirations, and long-term goals. Be creative. Build a picture of yourself as the perfect individual. You might even play some soothing music in the background as you record the script. It costs you nothing but a little effort to make it as long or short as you wish.

Unlike the so-called subliminal audio tapes, most of which have no message on them at all (and those which do cannot be consciously heard even with high-tech sound equipment), this kind of tape initially affects both the conscious and subconscious. Should you get "down" on yourself (as everyone does from time to time), play it to give yourself a lift by realizing and remembering all the positive qualities you possess and those yet to develop.

Play it as often as possible when you're alone, listening to it every day at home or in a car tape player. In a very short time, you'll notice that even while it's playing, the words will simply blend into the background and as you become less and less aware of the actual message it passes your conscious mind and goes directly into the subliminal more effectively than if you were consciously listening to it.

Subliminal Videotapes

Another method of positive reprogramming is the use of subliminal videotapes.

Unlike audio tapes, subliminal videotapes utilize imbeds which, barely perceptible to the human eye at normal speed, bypass conscious awareness and go directly to the subconscious, where they are easily identified. As mentioned previously, this method is so effective in modifying behavior that prohibition of the technology in advertising and promotion applications was supported by both the Bureau of Alcohol, Tobacco and Firearms and the FCC.

As a result, the sale of these tapes requires that the consumer be aware not only that they do include subliminal imbeds but also precisely what imbeds are used, which in high-quality tapes are visually evident in the frame-to-frame mode.

Subliminal videotapes are commercially available on topics ranging from stress reduction to weight and smoking control to success orientation, self-image, and the elimination of a variety of negative programming. Their manufacture is limited due to the high degree of technology required in production. (If you have difficulty locating a source, write to the Performance Dynamics address shown in "About the Author" at the end of this book.)

Used on a regular basis, the videotapes are highly effective and the results evident in modifying limiting programs in the subconscious, especially when used in conjunction with the variety of methods, both conscious and subliminal, described in this chapter.

Just as physical exercise and a proper diet bring about changes and improvements in your physique as long as you continue the program on a regular basis, subliminal fitness conditioning effects the same results in your subconscious.

Very slowly at first, you'll begin to notice subtle modifications in your behavior. You'll see a definite change in your attitude and a more positive approach to your job, other people, and your life in general. Decisions which were previously made based upon limiting programs will automatically be altered, guiding you toward different directions and therefore a new destiny which you may have always desired but could never achieve.

And like the results of any good physical conditioning program, subliminal fitness conditioning will make you feel good about yourself as a person and open doors to a future you never dreamed existed.

A future filled with the promise of . . .

DISCOVERY!

8

DISCOVERY

"Do not follow where the path may lead. Go instead where there is no path and leave a trail."—GEORGE BERNARD SHAW

There is no one exactly like you.

You are as unique and different from every person of the billions who populate this planet as one snowflake, one fingerprint is from another. Possessing motivations, qualities, hopes, dreams, aspirations, talents, abilities, and desires in combinations completely different from anyone else's in the whole wide world, you are as complex, complete, and perfect a creation as any in the universe.

But you are not alone, and you are not completely self-sufficient. Your accomplishments, setbacks, progress, and obstacles are the result of interaction with hundreds, even thousands who accompany you, some only momentarily and others continuing through the years on this exciting journey called life.

The purpose of this book is to give you a different perspective from which to view other people; to more accurately see things from their point of view; and to illustrate the thought processes which either hinder or propel their achievement.

But more importantly, in portraying others I hope it has given you a better insight into yourself.

Discovering the Secret

Before learning to effectively persuade, I spent years chasing what I wanted. The harder I chased, the more it eluded me, as is the case in so many things in life.

Once I learned how to persuade others effectively and consistently, however, I simultaneously discovered why the attainment of my desires had for so long been eluding me, always just out of reach. Because the ability of skilled persuasion imparts with it a secret.

To Get What You Want, Forget It!

If what you want—making the sale, getting the job, selling yourself, or "achieving your goal"—is foremost in your mind, it becomes obvious and counterproductive to efforts in dealing with other people.

Only when your concentration is sincerely and 100 percent on the fulfillment of their desires will you automatically achieve your own. Only by showing others how to be as successful as they want to be can you be successful; only by showing others how to get what they want can you get what you want; and only by learning how to effectively persuade others can you effectively persuade yourself.

What you have learned throughout these pages is not by any means the sum total of all the methods and techniques of persuasion. This book merely provides a foundation, a basis upon which to expand your knowledge and experience every day and in every situation for greater enrichment, fulfillment, excitement, and most importantly, fun in the adventure of life.

You have twenty-four-hour access to the most powerful computer in the world. It's called your mind. And when used properly, it will be your vehicle to places and achievement never before dreamed possible if you simply allow it to work for you.

Above all you need to be open, flexible, and willing to implement new thoughts, ideas, and attitudes in the face of criticism or negativity from those who are sure to tell you, "It can't be done" or "It's never been done that way before." Those are the people to avoid and ignore; who lack the progressive vision to see what can be instead of merely what has been; who will never reach tomorrow because their feet are so firmly planted in yesterday; and who, while claiming to strive for greatness, staunchly insist on embracing mediocrity.

There is no discovery, no excitement, and no profit in traveling the footworn path, thinking and doing and saying the same as everyone else has for generations. It is said that knowledge is the key to the door of success. But to open that door, it is first necessary to recognize the need to adapt to the only constant in the universe, which is change.

With that realization, you will receive a new and greater capacity: first to imagine, then to believe, and finally to innovate with the conviction and confidence that you have the ability and knowledge to succeed . . .

TO REACH OUT TO THE STARS!

BIBLIOGRAPHY AND RECOMMENDED READING

No single person, institution, or book, including *How 10% of the People Get 90% of the Pie,* represents the sum total of knowledge on any given subject.

As mentioned in the introduction, beginning with information based upon experience, we expanded that knowledge researching hundreds of books, tapes, and articles, then had the opportunity to field-test the methods and techniques we discovered and in some cases revised to learn which were the most effective to present to you, the reader, in the most concise form possible in these limited pages.

If you desire to grow in knowledge, to learn more for the enrichment of your life in a more in-depth approach than this or any single source can provide, we strongly recommend the following:

About Faces. Landau, Terry. New York: Doubleday, 1989.

The Age of Manipulation. Key, Wilson Bryan. New York: Henry Holt, 1989.

Applications of Neuro-Linguistic Programming. Dilts, Robert. Cupertino, CA: Meta Publications, 1983.

Awaken the Giant Within. Robbins, Anthony. New York: Summit Books, 1991.

A Better Way to Live. Mandino, Og. New York: Bantam Books, 1990.

Body Language. Fast, Juliet. New York: M. Evans, 1979.

The Greatest Salesman in the World. Mandino, Og. New York: Bantam Books, 1988.

Heart of the Mind. Andreas, Connirae. Moab, Utah: Real People Press, 1989.

Practical Magic. Lankton, Stephen R. Cupertino, CA: Meta Publications, 1980.

Real Magic, Creating Miracles in Everyday Life. Dyer, Wayne H. New York: Harper Collins, 1992.

Unlimited Power. Robbins, Anthony. New York: Simon and Schuster, 1986.

You'll See It When You Believe It. Dyer, Wayne H. New York: William Morrow, 1989.

About the Author

As a top marketing and sales executive with a number of major corporations, Craig E. Soderholm paid special attention to the behaviors of highly successful people. During this process, he discovered the incredible power of *subliminal persuasion* and spent several years researching and testing a variety of techniques he developed with amazing, consistent results.

Today, a consultant and co-founder of Performance Dynamics, his articles appear in international publications, and he conducts workshops and training programs on the art of Subliminal Power Persuasion.

As a result of those techniques, thousands of people have achieved financial success, professional achievement, and a higher level of personal fulfillment and accomplishment.

For additional information, please contact

PERFORMANCE DYNAMICS
P.O. Box 1311
Escondido, CA 92033-1311
Fax (760) 740-1785